Understanding the
SACRAMENTS
of VOCATION
A RITE-BASED APPROACH

RANDY STICE

LTP

LITURGY
TRAINING
PUBLICATIONS

Nihil Obstat
Reverend Daniel A. Smilanic, JCD
Vicar for Canonical Services
Archdiocese of Chicago
October 6, 2014

Imprimatur
Most Reverend Francis J. Kane, DD
Vicar General
Archdiocese of Chicago
October 6, 2014

The *Nihil Obstat* and *Imprimatur* are declarations that the material is free
from doctrinal or moral error, and thus is granted permission to publish in
accordance with c. 827. No legal responsibility is assumed by the grant of
this permission. No implication is contained herein that those who have
granted the *Nihil Obstat* and *Imprimatur* agree with the content, opinions,
or statements expressed.

UNDERSTANDING THE SACRAMENTS OF VOCATION: A RITE-BASED
APPROACH © 2016 Archdiocese of Chicago: Liturgy Training Publications,
3949 South Racine Avenue, Chicago, IL 60609; 1-800-933-1800;
fax 1-800-933-7094; e-mail orders@ltp.org; website www.ltp.org.

This book was edited by Kevin Thornton. Christian Rocha was the
production editor, Anna Manhart was the designer, and Juan Alberto
Castillo was the production artist.

Printed in the United States of America.

20 19 18 17 16   1 2 3 4 5

Library of Congress Control Number: 2016937061

ISBN: 978-1-61671-192-4

USV

CONTENTS

ABBREVIATIONS

CB — *Ceremonial of Bishops*

CCC — *Catechism of the Catholic Church*

CD — *Christus Dominus (Decree on the Pastoral Office of Bishops in the Church)*, Vatican Council II

DMLPD — *Directory for the Ministry and Life of Permanent Deacons*

DMLP — *Directory for the Ministry and Life of Priests*

EG — *Evangelium Gaudium (The Joy of the Gospel)*, Pope Francis

EM — *Eucharisticum Mysterium (Instruction on the Worship of the Eucharistic Mystery)*. Vatican Council II

FC — *Familiaris Consortio (On the Role of the Christian Family in the Modern World)*, St. John Paul II

GIL — *General Instruction of the Lectionary*

GILH — *General Instruction of the Liturgy of the Hours*

GIRM — *General Instruction of the Roman Missal*

GS — *Gaudium et Spes (Pastoral Constitution on the Church in the Modern World)*, Vatican Council II

HV — *Humanae Vitae (Of Human Life)*, Pope Paul VI

IOM — *Introduction to the Order of Mass*

LF — *Lumen Fidei (Light of Faith)*, Pope Francis

LG — *Lumen Gentium (Dogmatic Constitution on the Church)*, Vatican Council II

MND — *Mane Nobiscum Domine (Stay with Us Lord)*, Pope St. John Paul II

MS — *Musicam Sacram (Instruction on Music in the Liturgy)*, Vatican Council II

OCM — *Order of Christian Marriage*

PDV — *Pastores Dabo Vobis (I Will Give You Shepherds)*, Pope St. John Paul II

PCS — *Pastoral Care of the Sick*

PO — *Presbyterorum Ordinis (Decree on the Ministry and Life of Priests)*, Vatican Council II

RaP — *Reconciliation and Penance*, Apostolic Exhortation, Pope St. John Paul II

RBC — *Rite of Baptism for Children*

RM — *Roman Missal*, Third Typical Edition, 2011

RO — *Rites of Ordination*

RP — *Rite of Penance*

SacCar — *Sacramentum Caritatis*, Pope Benedict XVI

SC — *Sacrosanctum Concilium (Constitution on the Sacred Liturgy)*, Vatican Council II

STL — *Sing to the Lord: Music in Divine Worship*, United States Conference of Catholic Bishops

VD — *Verbum Domini (The Word of the Lord)*, Pope Benedict XVI

VL — *Varietates Legitimae (The Roman Liturgy and Inculturation)*, Congregation for Divine Worship and Discipline of the Sacraments

VQA — *Vicesimus Quintus Annus (On the 25th Anniversary of the Promulgation of the Conciliar Constitution "Sacrosanctum Concilium" on the Sacred Liturgy)*, Pope St. John Paul II

General Introduction

Before Jesus ascended to the Father, he promised the apostles that he would remain with them always. The seven sacraments of the Church—Baptism, Confirmation, Eucharist, Penance and Reconciliation, Anointing of the Sick, Holy Orders, Matrimony—are the primary ways that Jesus continues to fulfill the promise of his abiding presence. An encounter with the Trinity is the way the *Catechism of the Catholic Church* describes the sacraments: "A sacramental celebration is a meeting of God's children with their Father, in Christ and the Holy Spirit" (CCC, 1153). While various approaches and disciplines such as history, sociology, anthropology, psychology, semiotics, and ritual can deepen our understanding and experience of the sacraments, these approaches are secondary and build on what is primary—the personal encounter with the Trinity.

This Trinitarian sacramental encounter is a "dialogue" that uses both "actions and words" that together constitute "a language" (CCC, 1153). Like any language, this sacramental language has its own vocabulary, grammar, and syntax that must be learned if one is to enter into the sacramental dialogue with the Father in Christ and the Holy Spirit. The aim of this book is to explore and master the language of the sacraments, looking in detail at the sacraments of vocation—Holy Orders and Matrimony—so that we can participate fully, consciously and actively in this dialogue with the Trinity through the words and actions of the sacramental celebration.

TRINITARIAN

While Christ's institution of and action through the sacraments is rightly stressed, it is important to always remember and explore the Trinitarian dimension of the sacraments. "We are called to be a dwelling for the Most Holy Trinity: 'If a man loves me,' says the Lord, 'he will keep my word, and my Father will love him, and we will come to him, and make our home with him' [Jn 14:23]" (CCC, 260). The work of the Trinity in creation and salvation, what is known as "the divine economy," is performed jointly by the three divine persons, although each divine person contributes to the common work "according to his unique personal property" (CCC, 258). If we don't affirm the distinction of the persons, we deny that God is a trinity of persons, and if we don't affirm the unity and common work of the three persons, we profess three gods, not one. Throughout this volume I will delineate the activity of each divine person in the common work of the sacraments so that we can experience in our lives what the *Catechism* affirms, that "the whole Christian life is a communion with each of the divine persons, without in any way separating them" (CCC, 259).

TERMINOLOGY

In the course of this work you will encounter references not only to the sacraments but also to the liturgy, to liturgical celebrations as well as sacramental celebrations. The terms *liturgy* and *sacrament* are overlapping but not synonymous. *Liturgy* as it is used in this book is the more inclusive term, referring to the official public worship of the Church for which there are official ritual books. It includes the seven sacraments, but also such celebrations as the blessings found in the *Book of Blessings*, the *Liturgy of the Hours*, and the *Rite of Christian Initiation for Adults*. *Sacrament* is a narrower term that refers just to the seven sacraments of the Church. Everything said of the liturgy or liturgical celebrations is true of the sacraments, but references to the sacraments or sacramental celebrations are not necessarily true of non-sacramental liturgical celebrations such as those taken from the *Book of Blessings* or the *Liturgy of the Hours*. The *Catechism*'s summary concisely characterizes the relationship between the liturgy and the sacraments: "The whole liturgical life of the Church revolves around the Eucharistic sacrifice and the sacraments" (CCC, 1113).

Rite-Based

As the title indicates, my approach in this volume is rite-based. The rite itself is always the best starting point, for these are the words we hear and say, the gestures and postures we adopt, and the signs and symbols that engage us. In addition, the liturgy is one of the primary ways that the Church has passed on the faith entrusted to her by the Lord. Christ has entrusted to the Church the responsibility of passing "on the faith in its integrity so that the 'rule of prayer' (*lex orandi*) of the church may correspond to the 'rule of faith' (*lex credendi*)" (VL, 27). The terms "rule of prayer" (*lex orandi*) and "rule of faith" (*lex credendi*) refer to a principle that dates back to Prosper of Aquitaine (fifth century). "The law of prayer is the law of faith: the Church believes as she prays. Liturgy is a constitutive element of the holy and living Tradition" (CCC, 1124). St. Irenaeus (late second century), expressed this principle with respect to the Mass: "Our way of thinking is attuned to the Eucharist, and the Eucharist in turn confirms our way of thinking" (CCC, 1327). From the earliest days the Church has understood the inseparable relationship between her worship and her faith, and for this reason the sacramental rite is always the best starting point for understanding the meaning of the sacrament itself.

Sources

Since our approach is rite-based, our most important source will be the rite itself, which includes not only the words and actions of the rite but also the biblical readings for each of the sacraments. In addition, the *Roman Missal* contains ritual Masses for the celebration of the sacraments within the Mass (with the exception of the Sacrament of Penance and Reconciliation), and these texts (e.g., prayers, Prefaces, and Solemn Blessings) are also part of the sacramental rite. We will supplement the words and actions of the rite with selected other sources. The most frequently cited source is the *Catechism of the Catholic Church*, which St. John Paul II called "a sure and authentic reference text for teaching Catholic doctrine" and which he offered "to all the faithful who wish to deepen their knowledge of the unfathomable riches of salvation (cf. Eph 3:8)" (*Fidei Depositum*). Its presentation of the Catholic faith, illumined by Sacred Scripture, the writings of the saints, and the teaching of councils and popes, make it a rich and invaluable source of information on the sacraments. Readers of this book are encouraged to have a copy of the *Catechism of the Catholic Church* at hand. It is also available online at the Vatican website.

We will also make frequent reference to the documents of the Second Vatican Council (1962–1965), which made the reform and restoration of the liturgy its first priority in the *Constitution on the Sacred Liturgy (Sacrosanctum Concilium)*. The Council's *Dogmatic Constitution on the Church (Lumen Gentium)* is a key source in the discussion of the sacrament of Holy Orders, and the *Pastoral Constitution on the Church in the Modern World (Gaudium et Spes)* is similarly important in understanding the sacrament of Matrimony.[1] These foundational documents will be supplemented by papal writings such as St. John Paul II's apostolic exhortations *The Role of the Christian Family in the Modern World (Familiaris Consortio)* and *I Will Give You Shepherds (Pastores Dabo Vobis)* and Pope Benedict XVI's apostolic exhortation *The Word of the Lord (Verbum Domini)*. We will also have occasion to cite documents produced by Vatican congregations, such as the *Directory on the Ministry and Life of Priests* produced by the Congregation for the Clergy. Finally, we will listen to the saints, especially the Church Fathers from the early centuries of the Church, and we will also refer to works by contemporary theologians, liturgists, and historians.

As these sources suggest, we are not engaged in a speculative work of theology, nor are we proposing a new theory of the sacraments. Rather, our goal is to listen—attentively and prayerfully—to the voice of Christ and his Church in order to deepen our sacramental encounter with the Trinity.

Methodology

In this book we are using a method of sacramental catechesis described by Pope Emeritus Benedict XVI in his apostolic exhortation the *Sacrament of Charity (Sacramentum Caritatis)*. This type of catechesis is called *mystagogy*, from the Greek word for the person who led an initiate into a mystery. Its goal is to lead people from the signs of the sacrament to the spiritual realities they signify. Pope Emeritus Benedict XVI proposes looking at three aspects of a sacrament:

---

1. Most of the Second Vatican Council documents can also be found in *The Liturgy Documents*, vol. 1, 5th ed., and vol. 2, 2nd ed. (Chicago: Liturgy training Publications, 2012).

1. The Old Testament origins of the sacrament
2. The meaning of the signs and symbols which comprise the sacrament
3. The meaning of the sacrament for the whole of one's life (living the sacrament)

We will examine in detail each of these three aspects of the sacrament of Holy Orders and the sacrament of Matrimony by looking closely at the various elements of the rite and the different sources described above.

Organization

The book is divided into three parts. In part 1, we will briefly delve into an introduction to sacramental theology, consisting of chapters 1–3. Chapter 1 examines the different ways in which the Trinity is present in a sacramental celebration. Chapter 2 looks at the different sacramental signs that comprise the celebration. Chapter 3 introduces the method of mystagogical catechesis using examples from different sacraments to illustrate first the Old Testament roots, then the meaning of sacramental signs and symbols, and finally the comprehensive transformative power of the sacraments as we live sacramental lives. While the focus of this book is on the sacraments of vocation, the examples in part 1 are drawn from the sacraments of Baptism, Eucharist, Confirmation, Anointing of the Sick, and Reconciliation and Penance in order to provide the reader with some catechesis on all seven sacraments, not just the sacraments of Holy Orders and Matrimony.

Part 2 is a presentation of the Sacrament of Holy Orders. Chapter 4 traces the Old Testament origins of this sacrament, chapter 5 analyzes the signs and symbols of the sacrament, and chapter 6 explores the meaning of Holy Orders as a lived experience. Part 3 looks at the Sacrament of Matrimony, following the same structure as part 2: chapter 7 treats the Old Testament roots, chapter 8 examines the meaning of the constituent elements of the sacrament, and chapter 9 looks at the lived experience of the sacramental life. Chapter 10 concludes by discussing the sacraments of Holy Orders and Matrimony as sacraments at the service of communion.

AUDIENCE AND USE / ACTIVITIES

This book can be used by individuals as well as groups. It is primarily intended as a resource for those who are involved in preparing others for reception of the sacraments of Holy Orders or Matrimony. It is also appropriate for some religious education classes, adult faith formation, diaconate programs, undergraduate sacraments classes, and even high school sacraments classes. To facilitate its use in class or group settings, each chapter includes a number of different activities. These are intended to help the reader review and synthesize the material, explore a given topic in more detail (in some cases using the *Catechism of the Catholic Church*), and aid the reader in deepening his or her experience of the liturgy.

THE PRIVILEGED PLACE FOR ENCOUNTER

Although we encounter God in many different ways, "the Liturgy is the privileged place for the encounter of Christians with God and the one whom he has sent, Jesus Christ (cf. Jn 17:3)" (*Vicesimus Quintus Annus*, 7). It is there that "all Christian prayer finds its source and goal. Through the liturgy the inner man is rooted and grounded in 'the great love with which [the Father] loved us' in his beloved Son. It is the same 'marvelous work of God' that is lived and internalized by all prayer, 'at all times in the Spirit'" (CCC, 1073). It is my hope that this work will assist the reader in participating in the celebration of the sacraments of Holy Orders and Matrimony as privileged places of encounter with the Blessed Trinity, experiencing there the Father's love for us in Christ, poured into our hearts through the Holy Spirit.

PART I

Introduction to Sacramental Theology

This book is an introduction to the sacraments of vocation, Holy Orders and Matrimony. However, before looking in detail at these two sacraments, we will first consider the nature and power of the sacraments in general. The first three chapters of this volume present a concise introduction to sacramental theology—What is a sacrament? How does God act through the sacraments? How do the sacraments affect our lives? How can we enter more fully into each sacramental celebration?

The *Catechism of the Catholic Church* describes a sacramental celebration as "a meeting of God's children with their Father, in Christ and the Holy Spirit" (CCC, 1153). This is the fundamental conviction of this book: the sacraments are encounters with the Father in Christ and the Holy Spirit—the Trinity. We will begin by examining in chapter 1 how the sacraments fulfill Christ's promise to his apostles to be with them always. We will look particularly at how each person of the Trinity—Father, Son, and Holy Spirit—is present and active in a sacramental celebration. We will give special attention to how the sacraments make present the Passion, Death, Resurrection, and Ascension of Christ and how they dispense divine life to us (CCC, 1131).

The focus of chapter 2 is on the meeting of God with his children in a sacramental celebration that "takes the form of a dialogue, through actions and words," that is, through signs that comprise a sacramental language (CCC, 1153). Here we will look at several signs which are common to many or all of the sacraments: signs such as images, song, the Sign of the Cross, movement, incense, and color. Our discussion of these different sacramental signs will focus on how they are "bearers of the saving and sanctifying action of Christ," how the Spirit acts through these signs to impart to us the power of Christ's saving sacrifice to the praise and glory of God the Father (CCC, 1189).

In order for us to participate fully and fruitfully in sacramental celebrations, we must approach them with faith and understanding. The final chapter of this section describes an approach to liturgical catechesis that helps us do that. It has three elements. It begins by looking at the Old Testament roots of the sacrament, revealing the unity and progressive fulfillment of God's saving work that culminates in the person and work of Jesus Christ. Next, it analyzes the meaning of the different liturgical signs that comprise each sacrament. Finally, it considers the way each sacrament transforms our lives. In chapter 3 we will describe this method of catechesis and illustrate it with examples from the Sacraments of Initiation (Baptism, Eucharist, and Confirmation) and the Sacraments of Healing (Penance and Reconciliation and Anointing of the Sick). Taken together, these first three chapters will give us the foundation and tools for a detailed study of the Sacrament of Holy Orders and the Sacrament of Matrimony.

Chapter 1

The Sacraments: An Encounter with the Blessed Trinity

As Jesus was about to ascend to the Father, he gathered his disciples on the mountain. There he commanded them to "make disciples of all nations" and promised to be with them always: "And behold, I am with you always, until the end of the age" (Mt 28:19–20). Then "he parted from them and was taken up to heaven" (Lk 24:51). Luke tells us that the disciples experienced the Ascension with joy, not sadness: "they did him homage and then returned to Jerusalem with great joy" (Lk 24:52).

Why were the disciples joyful at Jesus' departure? Because they had experienced Christ's new way of being with them. Christ's sacramental presence is beautifully expressed in his encounter with the two disciples on the road to Emmaus who do not recognize him (Lk 24:13–35). After an introductory conversation (vv.13–24), "beginning with Moses and all the prophets, [Jesus] interpreted to them what referred to him in all the scriptures" (v. 27). The two disciples then invited him to stay with them, and they shared a meal. When Jesus was at table with them, "he took bread, said the blessing, broke it, and gave it to them" (v. 30)—these are Eucharistic actions. "With that their eyes were opened and they recognized him, but he vanished from their sight" (v. 31).

This account has the same structure as the Mass. It begins with the Liturgy of the Word—Jesus explaining to them how the Scriptures speak of him—and is followed by the Liturgy of the Eucharist, when Jesus took bread which he blessed, broke, and gave to them. At that moment he vanished from their sight, because he was now present in the Eucharist. This is Luke's way of explaining Jesus' new way of being with his disciples—his presence is now a sacramental presence, manifested through sacramental signs, preeminently through the signs of bread and wine. The *Catechism* explains the reason for Christ's new way of being with his disciples: "In this age of the Church Christ now lives and acts in and with his Church, in a new way appropriate to this new age" (CCC, 1076).Christ the Head is now present in and acts powerfully through his Body the Church, which "is like a sacrament (sign and instrument) in which the Holy Spirit dispenses the mystery of salvation" (CCC, 1111). Christ continues to proclaim the Kingdom of God through words and deeds, just as he did during his earthly ministry, only the manner is different—bodily in the time of the Gospels, now sacramentally through signs and symbols, words and actions, through his Body, the Church, in the liturgy. The *Catechism* explains how Christ acts through the sacraments by recalling healing miracles found in the Gospel according to Luke in which power came forth from Jesus to heal the sick. On one occasion, for example, a crowd was trying to touch Jesus, "because power came forth from him and healed them all" (Lk 6:19). On another occasion, a woman who had been sick for twelve years touched the fringe of his garment and was healed. Jesus instantly knew what had happened. He told Peter, "Someone has touched me; for I know that *power has gone out* from me" (8:46, italics added). These events prefigure what Christ now accomplishes through the sacraments: "Sacraments are *'powers that come forth'* from the Body of Christ, which is ever-living and life-giving" (CCC, 1116, italics added). All that Jesus did during his earthly ministry he continues to do today through the sacraments—*sacramentally*—"by means of signs perceptible to the senses" (SC, 7).

THE PASCHAL MYSTERY

There is a second reason why the disciples were joyful at his Ascension. Jesus was still with them and he had introduced a new presence and power into the world through his Paschal Mystery. Christ's Paschal Mystery (from the Greek noun *pascha*, which means "Passover," and the Greek verb *paschō*, which means "to suffer") refers to "his blessed passion, resurrection from the dead, and glorious ascension, whereby 'dying, he destroyed our death, and rising, restored our life'" (SC, 5). The Paschal Mystery is unique among all historical events: while all other historical events happen and then pass away, the Paschal Mystery "cannot remain only in the past, because by his death he destroyed death, and all that Christ is—all that he did and suffered for all men—participates in the divine eternity, and so transcends all times while being made present in them all. The event of the Cross and

Resurrection *abides* and draws everything toward life" (CCC, 1085). It is not just an event which we reverently remember, it is an ever-present reality "that the Church proclaims and celebrates in her liturgy so that the faithful may live from it and bear witness to it in the world" (CCC, 1068). It constitutes, wrote St. John Paul II, "the content of the daily life of the Church" (VQA, 6).

There is an integral connection between Jesus' earthly ministry and his Paschal Mystery. His words and actions during his earthly ministry anticipated in different ways the saving power of the Paschal Mystery that is now communicated through the Church in the liturgy (CCC, 1085). He himself was baptized by John in the Jordan, and he commanded his disciples to baptize new believers; he commissioned and empowered his followers to continue this ministry (Mt 28:18–20). He healed the sick and sent his disciples out to do the same (Mt 10:1). He forgave sinners and imparted the Spirit to the apostles to continue this ministry (cf. Jn 20:22–23). He celebrated the Last Supper with his disciples and commanded them to celebrate it often (Mt 26:26–29). He imparted to the Twelve a special power and authority to act in his name, and the apostles continued this in the early Church (Lk 24:49). In these events Christ announced and prepared what he would give the Church when all had been accomplished (Jn 19:30). "The mysteries of Christ's life are the foundations of what he would henceforth dispense in the sacraments, through the ministers of his Church" (CCC, 1115). In the memorable formulation of Pope St. Leo the Great (d. 461), "what was visible in our Savior has passed over into his mysteries [sacraments]" (CCC, 1115).

THE PASCHAL MYSTERY AND THE OTHER SACRAMENTS

All of the sacraments draw their power from the Paschal Mystery of Christ. "The Paschal Mystery is celebrated and made present in the liturgy of the Church, and its saving effects are communicated through the sacraments" (CCC, glossary). This is true in a preeminent way of the Eucharist, for "in the sacrifice of the Mass the passion of Christ is again made present" (RP, 2). However, it is also true of the other sacraments. For example, the *Rite of Baptism* explains the effects of Baptism: it is "the door to life and to the kingdom of God" (*General Introduction to*

Christian Initiation, 3); it incorporates recipients into the Church (ibid., 4); and it "washes away every stain of sin, original and personal, makes us sharers in God's own life and his adopted children" (ibid., 5). All of these effects are produced "by the power of the mystery of the Lord's passion and resurrection. . . . For baptism recalls and makes present the paschal mystery itself, because in baptism we pass from the death of sin into life" (ibid., 6).

The sacrament of Reconciliation also derives its power from the Paschal Mystery, for through the words of absolution, the imposition of hands, and the Sign of the Cross "the saving power of the passion, death and resurrection of Jesus is also imparted to the penitent as the 'mercy stronger than sin and offense'" (RaP, 31.III). Indeed, the words of absolution show "the connection between the reconciliation of the sinner and the paschal mystery of Christ" (RP, 19): "God, the Father of mercies, through the death and resurrection of his Son, has reconciled the world to himself. . . . " The *Catechism* summarizes the relationship between the Paschal Mystery and the sacraments as follows: "The Paschal Mystery is celebrated and made present in the liturgy of the Church, and its saving effects are communicated through the sacraments, especially the Eucharist, which renews the paschal sacrifice of Christ as the sacrifice offered by the Church" (CCC, glossary).

THE SACRAMENTS: THE WORK OF THE TRINITY

While Christ's role in the liturgy is rightly emphasized, it is important to remember that the Paschal Mystery is the work of the entire Trinity, as we read in the Letter to the Hebrews: "*Christ*, who through the eternal *spirit*, offered himself without blemish to *God*" (9:14, italics added). Indeed, everything accomplished by God in creation and salvation history is the joint work of the Trinity.[1] This is how St. Teresa of Avila explained it: "In all three Persons there is no more than one will, one power, and one dominion, in such a way that one cannot do anything without the others. . . . Could the Son create an ant without the Father? No, for it is all one power, and the same goes for the

---

1. "However, each divine person performs the common work according to his unique personal property" (CCC, 258).

Holy Spirit; thus there is only one all-powerful God and all three Persons are one Majesty."[2]

The sacraments are the work of the Trinity, for "a sacramental celebration is a meeting of God's children with their Father, in Christ and the Holy Spirit" (CCC, 1153). The Father is the source of blessing, which "is a divine and life-giving action" (CCC, 1078). "From the beginning until the end of time the whole of God's work is a *blessing*" (CCC, 1079). Examples of God's blessing include creation, his covenants with Noah and Abraham, the deliverance from Egypt, the gift of the promised land, God's presence in the Temple, and Israel's purifying exile and return (CCC, 1080–1081). However, it is in the liturgy that "the divine blessing is fully revealed and communicated" (CCC, 1082). Since the liturgy is a dialogue, we respond to the revelation and communication of the Father's blessing by rendering to him blessing and adoration for "all the blessings of creation and salvation with which he has blessed us in his Son, in order to give us the Spirit of filial adoption" (CCC, 1110).

Christ's action in the liturgy is to point to and make present through perceptible signs—his new, sacramental way of being with us—his own Paschal Mystery. He accomplishes this by manifesting his sacramental presence in a number of ways. He is present in the assembly in fulfillment of his promise that "where two or three are gathered together in my name, there am I in the midst of them" (Mt 18:20). He is also present in his ordained ministers, who are "sacramental signs of Christ" (CCC, 1087). He is present in his Word. And he is present "especially under the eucharistic elements" (SC, 7). Christ acts in the liturgy according to his new way of being with us, communicating to us the fruits of his Passion, Death, Resurrection, and Ascension.

The Holy Spirit, "teacher of the faith of the People of God and artisan of 'God's masterpieces,' the sacraments of the New Covenant" (CCC, 1091), acts in a number of ways in the liturgy. He prepares the people of God to receive Christ by awakening faith, conversion of heart, and adherence to the Father's will (CCC, 1098). He also recalls the mystery of Christ by "giving life to the Word of God," giving "a spiritual understanding of the Word of God," and giving "the grace of faith" to the listeners so that they may respond to the word in faith

---

2. Teresa of Avila, *The Collected Works of Teresa of Avila*, trans. Kieran Kavanaught, OCD, and Otilio Rodriguez, OCD, vol. 1, *The Book of Her Life, Spiritual Testimonies, Soliloquies* (Washington, DC: ICS Publications, 1976), 401.

(CCC, 1100–1102). The Spirit also makes present the Paschal Mystery of Christ through his "transforming power in the liturgy (CCC, 1107). Finally, the Holy Spirit, "who is the Spirit of communion," brings the assembly into communion with Christ, forming them into his Body (CCC, 1108). The section of the *Catechism* (1091–1109) on the Holy Spirit in the liturgy is worth a careful and prayerful reading, for it "makes a remarkable contribution to a new Trinitarian understanding of the liturgy."[3]

The presence and work of the Trinity is beautifully expressed in Eucharistic Prayer III: "You are indeed Holy, O *Lord* . . . for through your Son our Lord *Jesus Christ*, by the power and working of the *Holy Spirit*, you give life to all things and make them holy" (italics added). God the Father, through the Son, by the power and working of the Holy Spirit, gives life and sanctifies all things. The Sacrament of Penance is also an encounter with the Trinity, for the words and gestures of absolution constitute "the moment at which, in response to the penitent, the Trinity becomes present in order to blot out sin and restore innocence" (RaP, 31.III). Thus, every sacramental celebration is an action of the three Persons of the Trinity and draws us ever more deeply into the mystery of Trinitarian love.

THE NATURE OF THE LITURGY

Before considering in more detail the sacraments as works of the Trinity, we need to look briefly at the nature of the liturgy. In the *Constitution on the Sacred Liturgy* the Second Vatican Council described the liturgy in the following terms:

> Rightly, then, the liturgy is considered as an exercise of the priestly office of Jesus Christ. In the liturgy, by means of signs perceptible to the senses, human sanctification is signified and brought about in ways proper to each of these signs; in the liturgy the whole public worship is performed by the Mystical Body of Jesus Christ, that is, by the Head and his members.
>
> From this it follows that every liturgical celebration, because it is an action of Christ the Priest and of his Body which is the Church, is a sacred action surpassing all others; no other action of the Church can equal its effectiveness by the same title and to the same degree. (SC, 7)

---

3. Francis Eugene Cardinal George, OMI, "*Sacrosanctum Concilium* Anniversary Address: The Foundations of Liturgical Reform," in *Cardinal Reflections: Active Participation and the Liturgy* (Chicago: Hillenbrand Books, 2005), 47.

This description makes three important assertions.

- First, the liturgy is "an exercise of the priestly office of Jesus Christ," which means that he is the celebrant at every liturgy.
- Second, Christ is present in the liturgy through "signs perceptible to the sense" and he works "in ways proper to each of these signs." This is what we mean when we speak of Christ being present and acting *sacramentally*—he is truly present, but now through "signs perceptible to the senses."
- Third, the liturgy "is performed by the Mystical Body of Jesus Christ, that is, by the Head and his members." Christ is manifested sacramentally as Body and Head in distinct ways.

CHRIST IS PRESENT, HEAD AND BODY

Christ's presence in his Mystical Body is a fulfillment of his promise to his disciples: "Where two or three are gathered together in my name, there am I in the midst of them" (Mt 18:20). Although this presence is manifested in different ways, we will look at only one example. In the Eucharist it is accomplished through the celebrant's Greeting—"The Lord be with you"—and the people's response—"And with your spirit." The celebrant's greeting "signifies the presence of the Lord to the assembled community" (GIRM, 50). Together with the people's response, "the mystery of the Church gathered together is made manifest" (GIRM, 50). In other words, through this simple dialogue, a profound change takes place—the congregation has become a new sacramental reality—it has become the Mystical Body of Christ gathered in this place, making visibly present the mystery of the Church. It is no longer just a group of people gathered in one place; now it is the Body of Christ prepared to perform the public worship of the Church.

The greeting and response also make sacramentally visible Christ the Head. According to the *Catechism of the Catholic Church*, "Through the ordained ministry, especially that of bishops and priests, the presence of Christ as head of the Church is made visible in the midst of the community" (CCC, 1549).

In the Eucharist, this visible presence of Christ as head is manifested especially through the people's response, "And with your spirit." This is more than a simple greeting along the lines of "and also with you"; it is a reference to the gift of the Spirit received at ordination. This understanding of the people's response is very ancient. In the fifth century, Narsai of Nisibis explained that "spirit" refers "not to the soul of the priest but to the Spirit he has received through the laying on of hands."[4] It is only through the gift of the Spirit received at ordination that the liturgy is able to go forward. In the words of a contemporary scholar, "The community's response could be understood as a short intercession for its president, that he may fulfill well his role as president with the help of the Lord and in the ministerial grace bestowed by his Spirit."[5] The Church also urges the priest to make this sacramental reality apparent through his celebration of the Mass: "by his bearing and by the way he pronounces the divine words he must convey to the faithful the living presence of Christ" (GIRM, 93).

THE WORD OF GOD

Christ is also present in his Word. When the Holy Scriptures are proclaimed in the liturgy, it is "he himself who speaks" (SC, 7). Christ is present through his Word in multiple ways in the liturgy. First, "it is from Scripture that the readings are given and explained in the homily and that psalms are sung." Second, "the prayers, collects, and liturgical songs are *scriptural in their inspiration*" (italics added). Third, "it is from the Scriptures that actions and signs derive their meaning" (SC, 24). Christ the eternal Word proclaims his Word in the liturgical assembly, his Word gives the prayers and liturgical text their unique power, and it interprets the signs and actions that comprise the liturgy.

Indeed, there is an intrinsic unity between God's deeds and words. "In salvation history there is no separation between what God *says* and what he *does*. His word appears as alive and active (cf. Heb 4:12)" (VD, 53). God created through his word: "God said: Let there be light, and there was light" (Gn 1:3). This same power is evident in many of Jesus' miracles. Jesus said to the paralytic, "I say to you, rise, pick up your mat, and go home" (Mk 2:11), and he was immediately healed. When Jesus and his disciples were engulfed in a storm at sea, Jesus

---

4. Robert Cabie, *The Eucharist*, trans. Matthew J. O'Connell, in *The Church at Prayer*, vol. 2 (Collegeville, MN: The Liturgical Press, 1986), 51.

5. Michael Kunzler, *The Church's Liturgy,* trans. Placid Murray, OSB, Henry O'Shea, OSB, and Cilian Ó Sé, OSB (London: Continuum, 2001), 198.

rebuked the wind and said to the sea, "Quiet! Be still!"(Mk 4:39). The wind immediately ceased and a great calm prevailed. Pope Benedict XVI calls this the "performative character" of God's word, which is not confined to the past, but is a present reality. "In the liturgical action too, we encounter his word which accomplishes what it says" (VD, 53).

The performative character of the Word of Christ in the liturgy is supremely evident in the Eucharist when the priest pronounces the words of Christ over the bread and wine. This is how St. John Chrysostom (d. 407) explained this mystery: "The priest, in the role of Christ, pronounces these words, but their power and grace are God's. This is my body, he says. This word transforms the things offered" (CCC, 1375).[6] Sixteen hundred years later, St. John Paul II affirmed this same reality. It is the priest "who says with the power coming to him from Christ in the Upper Room: 'This is my body which will be given up for you. . . . This is the cup of my blood, poured out for you . . . .' The priest says these words, or rather *he puts his voice at the disposal of the One who spoke these words in the Upper Room . . .* " (*Ecclesia de Eucharistia*, 5). God's Word is efficacious, accomplishing what it signifies.

The Word of God proclaimed in the liturgy "is always a living and effective word through the power of the Holy Spirit. It expresses the Father's love that never fails in its effectiveness towards us" (VD, 52). The Word of the Father is made present and personal through the action of the Holy Spirit. "In the word of God proclaimed and heard, and in the sacraments, Jesus says today, here and now, to each person: 'I am yours, I give myself to you'; so that we can receive and respond, saying in return: 'I am yours'" (VD, 51). Understanding the performative character of God's Word in the liturgy can help us recognize God's activity in salvation history and in our own lives (VD, 53), acting at times in ways that surprise and amaze us, for as Pope Francis reminds us, "God's word is unpredictable in its power." (EG, 22).

---

6. It is the constant teaching of the Church that the bread and wine are transformed into the Body and Blood of Christ *through the Word of Christ and the working of the Holy Spirit*: "The Church Fathers strongly affirmed the faith of the Church in the efficacy of the Word of Christ and of the action of the Holy Spirit to bring about this conversion" (CCC, 1375).

> ### Digging into the Catechism
>
> The reading of the Gospel during Mass is accompanied by a rich variety of sacramental signs. What are the different signs that accompany this key moment of the Mass? (Cf. CCC, 1154)

INVOKING THE HOLY SPIRIT: THE EPICLESIS

One of the essential elements in every sacramental celebration is the invocation of the Holy Spirit. This invocation is called the *epiclesis*, from the Greek word meaning "to call upon." Every sacrament includes an epiclesis, a "prayer asking for the sanctifying power of God's Holy Spirit" (CCC, glossary). It is accompanied by a gesture dating back to the Apostles: "The life-giving power of the Spirit, who moved over the waters in the first days of creation and overshadowed Mary in the moment of the incarnation, is vividly expressed by the ancient gesture of bringing together the hands with the palms downward and extended over the elements to be consecrated" (IOM, 118).

Let's look at a few examples. In the sacrament of Baptism there is an epiclesis over the baptismal water. This epiclesis reads as follows:

> May the power of the Holy Spirit,
> O Lord, we pray,
> come down through your Son
> into the fullness of this font,
> so that all who have been buried with Christ
> by Baptism into death
> may rise again to life with him.
> Who lives and reigns with you in the unity of the Holy Spirit,
> one God, for ever and ever.
>
> R. Amen. (RM, Easter Vigil, Blessing of Baptismal Water)

Another example is the consecration of the sacred holy oil, chrism. The epiclesis for the consecration of sacred chrism by the bishop at the Chrism Mass during Holy Week is expressed in the following words: "And so, Father, we ask you to bless ✚ this oil you have created. Fill it with the power of your Holy Spirit through Christ your Son. Make this Chrism a sign of life and salvation for those who are to be born again in the waters of Baptism. Through this sign of Chrism grant them royal, priestly, and prophetic honor, and clothe with them incorruption" (*Rite of Consecration of Chrism*). In the Mass we find two epicleses. The first, spoken over the bread and wine to change them into the Body and Blood of Christ, is called the consecratory epiclesis. The second epiclesis, invoked over the congregation, is called the communion epiclesis, because it asks "that those who take part in the Eucharist may be one body and one spirit" (CCC, 1353). The epiclesis is an essential element of every liturgical celebration, ensuring that "there is an outpouring of the Holy Spirit that makes the unique mystery present" (CCC, 1104).

LITURGICAL REMEMBERING: THE ANAMNESIS

The second element "at the heart of each sacramental celebration" (CCC, 1106) is the anamnesis. The word itself is a transliteration of a Greek word that is translated as "reminder" or "remembrance." It occurs twice in the earliest account of the Last Supper, 1 Corinthians 11:23–26, written by St. Paul in the mid-50s. Jesus' words over the bread (11:24) and the cup (11:25) conclude with the command to "do this . . . in remembrance [anamnesis] of me." The anamnesis, the "remembrance" or "memorial," is "a living re-presentation before God of the saving deeds he has accomplished in Christ, so that their fullness and power may be effective here and now" (IOM, 121).

The anamnesis or remembrance "is not merely the recollection of past events but the proclamation of the mighty works wrought by God for men. In the liturgical celebration of these events, *they become in a certain way present and real.* This is how Israel understands its liberation from Egypt: every time Passover is celebrated, the Exodus events are made present to the memory of believers so that they may conform their lives to them" (CCC, 1363, italics added). "In the New Testament, the memorial takes on new meaning. When the Church celebrates the Eucharist, she commemorates Christ's Passover, and *it is made present*: the sacrifice Christ offered once for all on the cross remains ever present. 'As often as the sacrifice of the Cross by which "Christ our Pasch has been sacrificed" is celebrated on the altar, the work of our redemption is carried out'" (CCC, 1364, italics added).

In the Rite of Baptism the anamnesis is found in the Prayer over the Water: "O God, whose Son, baptized by John in the waters of the

Jordan, was anointed with the Holy Spirit, and, *as he hung upon the Cross, gave forth water from his side along with blood, and after his Resurrection,* commanded his disciples: 'Go forth, teach all nations, baptizing them in the name of the Father and of the Son and of the Holy Spirit.'" (RM, Easter Vigil, Blessing of Baptismal Water; italics added). In the Mass, every Eucharistic Prayer contains an anamnesis "in which the Church calls to mind the Passion, Resurrection, and glorious return of Christ Jesus" (CCC, glossary). The anamnesis always comes after the words of institution and is followed by the oblation, in which the Church "presents to the Father the offering of his Son which reconciles us with him" (CCC, 1354). In Eucharistic Prayer III the anamnesis, offering, and thanksgiving or doxology are expressed eloquently and concisely: "Therefore, O Lord, as we celebrate the memorial of the saving Passion of your Son, his wondrous Resurrection and Ascension into heaven, and as we look forward to his second coming [anamnesis], we offer you [offering] in thanksgiving [doxology] this holy and living sacrifice."

THE REAL PRESENCE—PAR EXCELLENCE

Finally, Christ is present in the Eucharistic species in a manner that is utterly unique and "raises the Eucharist above all the sacraments as 'the perfection of the spiritual life and the end to which all the sacraments tend'" (CCC, 1374). In the Eucharistic species "the body and blood, together with the soul and divinity, of our Lord Jesus Christ and, therefore, *the whole Christ is truly, really, and substantially* contained" (CCC, 1374): truly, "not simply through image or form," really, "not only subjectively through the faith of believers," and substantially, "in his profound reality, which cannot be seen by the senses, and not in the appearances which remain that of bread and wine."[7] In affirming the real presence of Christ in the Eucharistic species the Church is not denying Christ's real presence in other ways. Rather, his presence in the Eucharistic species "is presence in the fullest sense: that is to say, it is a *substantial* presence by which Christ, God and man, makes himself wholly and entirely present" (CCC, 1374). The Eucharist, therefore, contains "the entire spiritual wealth of the church, namely Christ himself our Pasch" (PO, 5).

---

7. Raniero Cantalamessa, *The Eucharist: Our Sanctification*, rev. ed. (Collegeville, MN: The Liturgical Press, 1995), 81.

This presence is expressed in several ways in the words of the Mass. In the Liturgy of the Eucharist, the Preface, Eucharistic Prayer, and Our Father are all addressed to God the Father. However, the prayers following the Our Father are addressed to Christ, now substantially present on the altar. Immediately following the Our Father the priest addresses Christ: "Lord Jesus Christ, who said to your apostles . . . " This is followed by the "Lamb of God," which is also addressed to Christ, now substantially present on the altar. Finally, the priest shows the consecrated host and blood and says, "Behold the Lamb of God, behold him who takes away the sins of the world" (RM, Order of Mass, 132). We do not behold "It", a holy thing, but the person of Christ, the Son of God, under the appearance of bread. Sacramental communion also has the character of a personal encounter. For this reason, "ordained ministers and those who . . . are authorized to exercise the ministry of distributing the Eucharist [should] make every effort to ensure that this simple act preserves its importance as a personal encounter with the Lord Jesus in the sacrament" (Benedict XVI, SacCar, 50).

St. Teresa of Avila expressed the reality of Christ's presence in the Eucharist with particularly vivid and personal language: "Receiving Communion is not like picturing with the imagination. . . . In Communion the event is happening now, and it is entirely true. . . . Now, then, if when He went about in the world the mere touch of His robes cured the sick, why doubt, if we have faith, that miracles will be worked while He is within us and that He will give what we ask of Him, since He is in our house? His Majesty is not accustomed to paying poorly for His lodging if the hospitality is good."[8]

Finally, the presence of Christ in the liturgy is manifested through the signs and symbols which make up the liturgical rites. Through the power of the Spirit, they "become *bearers of the saving and sanctifying action of Christ*" (CCC, 1189, italics added). They comprise the language of the liturgy, which is the subject of the next chapter.

---

8. Teresa of Avila, *The Collected Works of Teresa of Avila*, trans. Kieran Kavanaugh, OCD, and Otilio Rodriguez, OCD, vol. 2, *The Way of Perfection, Meditations on the Song of Sons, The Interior Castle* (Washington, DC: ICS Publications, 1980), 172.

Digging into the Rite of Reconciliation and Penance

Which of the elements of presence do you find in the formula of absolution from the Rite of Penance?

Then the priest extends his hands over the head of the penitent (or at least extends his right hand):

> God, the Father of mercies,
> through the death and resurrection of his Son,
> has reconciled the world to himself
> and sent the Holy Spirit among us
> for the forgiveness of sins;
> through the ministry of the Church
> may God give you pardon and peace,
> and **I absolve you from your sins**
> **in the name of the Father,**
> **and of the Son, ✝ and of the Holy Spirit.** (RP, 46)

Chapter 2

The Language of the Liturgy

The liturgy is composed of signs and symbols through which God manifests his presence as well as his saving and sanctifying action. He mediates his presence through signs and symbols because this corresponds to our very nature, to the way he created us. We are both body and spirit, so we express and perceive "spiritual realities through physical signs and symbols" (CCC, 1146). In addition, because we have been created as social beings, we need "signs and symbols to communicate with others, through language, gestures, and actions" (CCC, 1146). This is equally true of our relationship with God. "For in God's design the humanity and loving kindness of our Savior have visibly appeared to us and so God uses visible signs to give salvation and to renew the broken covenant" (RP, 6d).

The signs of the liturgy confer salvation and renew the broken covenant because they are "bearers of the saving and sanctifying action of Christ" (CCC, 1189). Their power stems from their origin: "the visible signs used by the liturgy to signify invisible divine things have been chosen by Christ or the Church" (SC, 33). Examples of signs chosen by Christ include unleavened bread and grape wine for the Eucharist, the use of oil for the Anointing of the Sick, and the baptismal formula "in the name of the Father and of the Son and of the Holy Spirit." Signs chosen by the Church include liturgical vestments and colors, postures such as standing and kneeling, and gestures such as the Sign of the Cross. These signs, whether chosen by Christ or the Church, are bearers of the power of Christ's Paschal Mystery in a way that is not possible with signs chosen by us. Furthermore, they are "needed for the fulfillment of the mystery of salvation in the Christian community" and to ensure the presence of God (*Liturgiae Instaurationes*, 1). Through signs the liturgy makes present the transforming power of Christ's Paschal Mystery, bringing us into relationship with the Trinity.

When the Church speaks of liturgical signs, she uses the term in a broad and comprehensive way, including material objects, words, actions, song, and music. They are drawn from elements and actions "relating to creation (candles, water, fire), human life (washing, anointing, breaking bread) and the history of salvation (the rites of the Passover)" (CCC, 1189). All of the liturgical signs and symbols are related to Christ and find their fulfillment in him. When we talk about liturgical signs and symbols, the distinction between sign and symbol is not the important point: "what is important is that, whichever term is employed—be it 'sign' or 'symbol'—the meaning each has for the Church is one of fullness, reality, and truth. In fact, that to which signs and symbols point is *the* fullness, reality, and truth: Christ himself"[1]. The Trinity acts through the liturgical signs: the Holy Spirit uses the words, actions, and signs that make up a liturgical celebration to put "both the faithful and the ministers into a living relationship with Christ, the Word and Image of the Father, so that they can live out the meaning of what they hear, contemplate, and do in the celebration" (CCC, 1101). Through the faith of the Church and the power of the Holy Spirit, God communicates the fruits of Christ's Paschal Mystery to us by means of this liturgical language.

There is a close relationship between the power of liturgical signs and their intelligibility. The intelligibility of the signs and symbols of the liturgy was a primary concern of the Second Vatican Council in its reform of the liturgy. "It is therefore of the highest importance that the faithful should readily understand the sacramental signs" (SC, 59) so that they can "take part in the rites fully, actively, and as befits a community" (SC, 21). Intelligible signs enable the liturgy to enter "surely and effectively . . . [into] the minds and lives of the faithful" (EM, 4). When misunderstood, the language of the liturgy can be confusing or meaningless, but when understood it is inexhaustibly rich, varied and powerful.

SACRAMENTAL SIGNS AND SYMBOLS

Sacramental signs are different from the signs that we encounter in our daily life. For example, a hospital sign indicates the location of a hospital, but it does not contain the hospital itself. It is merely an indicator, a pointer. Sacramental signs also point to another reality, but unlike conventional signs, they also make present the reality they signify. "The

---

1. Christopher Carstens and Douglas Martis, *Mystical Body, Mystical Voice: Encountering Christ in the Words of the Mass* (Chicago: Liturgy Training Publications, 2011), 40.

liturgical word and action are inseparable both insofar as they are signs and instruction and insofar as *they accomplish what they signify*. When the Holy Spirit awakens faith, he not only gives an understanding of the Word of God, but *through the sacraments also makes present the 'wonders' of God* which it proclaims" (CCC, 1155, italics added). This reality is expressed in the liturgy itself. Consider, for example, the Prayer after Communion for the Thirtieth Sunday in Ordinary Time: "May your Sacraments, O Lord, we pray, perfect in us what lies within them, that what we now celebrate in signs we may one day possess in truth." God uses the signs and symbols of the liturgy to communicate the power and reality of the Paschal Mystery to us.

Through the richness and diversity of its signs, the liturgy engages the whole person: mind, body, and senses. It engages the hearing through words and song; smell through incense; sight through vestments, images, colors; feeling through posture and gesture; and taste through the Body and Blood of Christ under the appearance of bread and wine. Through these different "kinds of language," the liturgy operates "on different levels of communication" and engages the whole person (SacCar, 40) so that each participant can enter into the liturgy with his or her whole being.

Let us now consider some of the signs common to all of the sacraments. We looked at a few liturgical signs in the previous chapter, such as the liturgical word and the gesture that accompanies the invocation of the Holy Spirit. In this chapter we will consider additional signs and symbols that are common to many of the Church's sacramental celebrations: images, song, the Sign of the Cross, silence, movement, incense, and color. Finally, we will consider the importance of the harmony of the liturgical signs.

Images

An element common to all Catholic churches, and therefore a part of every liturgical celebration, is the liturgical image. Sacred art is a direct consequence of the Incarnation. No image can "represent the invisible and incomprehensible God, but the incarnation of the Son of God has ushered in a new 'economy' of images" (CCC, 1159). St. John Damascene explained this new "economy of images" in the seventh century: "Previously God, who has neither a body nor a face, absolutely could not be represented by an image. But now that he has made himself visible in the flesh and has lived with men, I can make an image of what I have seen of God . . . and contemplate the glory of the Lord, his face unveiled" (CCC, 1159). The sacred image and sacred word teach and reinforce the one Gospel message of Jesus Christ. In 787, the Second Council of Nicaea affirmed this reciprocal relationship between Sacred Scripture and sacred art: "the production of representational artwork . . . accords with the history of the preaching of the Gospel. For it confirms that the incarnation of the Word of God was real and not imaginary, and to our benefit as well, for realities that illustrate each other undoubtedly reflect each other's meaning" (CCC, 1160, quoting the Council of Nicaea II, 787).

Sacred images "truly signify Christ, who is glorified in them" (CCC, 1161), and in a certain way make present an integral aspect of every sacramental celebration, the "cloud of witnesses" spoken of in Hebrews 12:1, "who continue to participate in the salvation of the world and to whom we are united, above all in sacramental celebrations" (CCC, 1161). This heavenly dimension was reaffirmed by the Second Vatican Council: "In the earthly liturgy we take part in a foretaste of that heavenly liturgy celebrated in the holy city of Jerusalem toward which we journey as pilgrims, where Christ is sitting at the right hand of God, a minister of the holies and of the true tabernacle; we sing a hymn to the Lord's glory with the whole company of heaven" (SC, 8). Sacramental celebrations unite heaven and earth, joining us with the entire heavenly host, as evidenced, for example, in the invocation of the Penitential Rite: "I ask blessed Mary ever-Virgin, all the Angels and Saints, and you, my brothers and sisters" (RM, *Confiteor*).

This heavenly, vertical dimension of the liturgy is deeply rooted in our tradition. In the fifth century St. John Chrysostom described the angelic presence at the Eucharist: "The angels surround the priest. The whole sanctuary and the space around the altar are filled with the heavenly powers to honor Him Who is present on the altar."[2] Three centuries later St. Bede (d. 735) exhorted the faithful in the following words: "We are not permitted to doubt that where the mysteries of the Lord's body and blood are being enacted, a gathering of the citizens from on high is present. . . . Hence we must strive meticulously, my brothers, when we come into the church to pay the due service of divine praise or

---

2. Jean Daniélou, SJ, *The Angels and Their Mission*, trans. David Heimann (Westminster, MD: The Newman Press, 1956), 62.

to perform the solemnity of the mass, to be always mindful of the angelic presence, and to fulfill our heavenly duty with fear and fitting veneration."[3] In a real and powerful way heaven becomes present on earth at every liturgical celebration.

Sacred images are an integral part of the liturgy, for they help us perceive the heavenly host present with us at every liturgical celebration. "Images point to a presence; they are essentially connected with what happens in the liturgy. Their whole point is to lead us beyond what can be apprehended at the merely material level, to awaken new senses in us, and to teach us *a new kind of seeing*, which perceives the Invisible in the visible."[4] Sacred images help us to "look not to what is seen but to what is unseen; for what is seen is transient, but what is unseen is eternal" (2 Cor 4:18). Every liturgical celebration is a participation in the heavenly liturgy eternally celebrated in the heavenly Jerusalem. Sacred images assist us in understanding and entering into this vital aspect of the liturgy.

Song

Music, as with all liturgical signs, manifests the presence of God, for "God, the giver of song, is present whenever his people sing his praises" (STL, 1). It enriches the liturgy in a variety of ways. Prayer, when sung, has "a more graceful expression" (MS, 5). Song also manifests more clearly the "hierarchic character of the liturgy and the specific make-up of the community," since different parts of the liturgy are sung by the priest celebrant (the prayers/orations, the preface), the cantor (the responsorial psalm), the *schola* or choir, and the entire assembly (e.g., the Kyrie, the Gloria, and the Entrance chant) (MS, 5). The union of voices contributes to the "union of hearts," one of the ways that we, though many, are one body in Christ. Also, song "raises the mind more readily to heavenly realities through the splendor of the rites" (MS, 5). St. John Chrysostom emphasized this dimension in the exhortation "Lift up your hearts": "Let no one have any thought of earth, but let him lose himself of every earthly thing and transport himself whole and entire into heaven. Let him abide there beside the very throne of glory,

---

3. Erik M. Heen and Philip D.W. Krey, eds, *Hebrews*, Ancient Christian Commentary on Scripture (Downers Grove, IL: InterVarsity Press, 2005), 30.

4. Joseph Ratzinger, *The Spirit of the Liturgy*, trans. John Saward (San Francisco: Ignatius, 2000), 133 (italics added).

hovering with the Seraphim, and singing the most holy song of the God of glory and majesty."[5]

As we noted above, the earthly liturgy is a participation in the heavenly liturgy. Music is an important aspect of that participation. In the words of the Second Vatican Council, "we sing a hymn to the Lord's glory with the whole company of heaven" (SC, 8). St. John Chrysostom described this dimension of the liturgy: "Think now of what kind of choir you are going to enter. Although vested with a body, you have been judged worthy to join the Powers of heaven in singing the praises of Him who is Lord of all."[6] Music and song, along with sacred images, manifest the heavenly dimension of the earthly liturgy. Through song, the whole liturgy becomes "a more striking symbol of the celebration to come in the heavenly Jerusalem" (MS, 5).

Music in the liturgy is a rich and powerful bearer of the saving and sanctifying power of Christ in many ways. It enhances prayer. It manifests the mystery of the Church, which is simultaneously hierarchical and unified. It helps us set our mind on heavenly things. Through song we join the heavenly choir that never ceases to sing the praises of God (Rev 4:8). Liturgical song is "a sign of God's love for us and of our love for him" (STL, 2), one of the sacramental signs through which we are brought into unity with the Trinity and with one another, are made holy, and give glory to God.

The Sign of the Cross

Gestures are another kind of liturgical sign. Perhaps the one that is most common and familiar to every sacramental celebration is the Sign of the Cross. This is a very ancient Christian gesture. Tertullian (ca. 200) saw the Sign of the Cross prefigured in Ezekiel 9:4, in which the Lord instructed the prophet to go through Jerusalem and mark on the forehead those "who grieve and lament over all the abominations practiced within it." Here is Tertullian's explanation:

> [Christ] foretold that His just ones should suffer equally with Him—both the apostles and all the faithful in succession; and He signed them with that very seal of which Ezekiel spake: "The Lord said unto me, go through the gate, through the midst of Jerusalem, and set the mark *Tau* upon the

---

5. Daniélou, *Angels,* 62.

6. Ibid.

foreheads of the men." Now the Greek letter *Tau* and our own letter T is the very form of the cross, which He predicted would be the sign on our foreheads in the true Catholic Jerusalem, in which, according to the twenty-first Psalm, the brethren of Christ or children of God would ascribe glory to God the Father, in the person of Christ Himself addressing His Father: "I will declare Your name unto my brethren; in the midst of the congregation will I sing praise unto Thee."[7]

He also describes how frequently it was made by the early Christians: "At every forward step and movement, at every going in and out, when we put on our clothes and shoes, when we bathe, when we sit at table, when we light the lamps, on couch, on seat, in all the ordinary actions of daily life, we trace upon the forehead the sign."[8] Through the Sign of the Cross, prefigured in Old Testament prophecy and fulfilled in Christ, Christians proclaim their fidelity to the thrice-holy God, symbolized by the sign of the cross.

A century and a half later, St. Cyril of Jerusalem explained the Sign of the Cross to the newly-baptized Christians. It is, first of all, a confession of faith: "Let us not then be ashamed to confess the Crucified. Be the Cross our seal made with boldness by our fingers on our brow, and on everything."[9] It was still used by Christians to sanctify the moments and events of daily life: "over the bread we eat, and the cups we drink; in our comings in, and goings out; before our sleep, when we lie down and when we rise up; when we are in the way, and when we are still."[10] St. Cyril also describes the power of the sign of the cross to keep Christians safe against the wiles and attacks of the enemy: "Great is that preservative; it is without price, for the sake of the poor; without toil, for the sick; since also its grace is from God. It is the Sign of the faithful, and the dread of devils: for He triumphed over them in it, having made a show of them openly [Col 2:15]; for when they see the Cross they are reminded of the Crucified; they are afraid of

---

7. Tertullian, *Against Marcion*, in vol. 3 of *The Ante-Nicene Fathers: Translations of The Writings of the Fathers Down to AD 325*, ed. Alexander Roberts, DD, and James Donaldson, LLD. (Grand Rapids, MI: Eerdmans Publishing Company, 1980), 340–341.

8. Tertullian, *De Corona*, in vol. 3 of *The Ante-Nicene Fathers: Translations of The Writings of the Fathers Down to AD 325*, ed. Alexander Roberts, DD, and James Donaldson, LLD. (Grand Rapids, MI: Eerdmans Publishing Company, 1980), 94–95.

9. Cyril of Jerusalem, "Catechetical Lectures, Lecture XIII," in *A Select Library of Nicene and Post-Nicene Fathers of the Christian Church*, Second Series, vol. 7, ed. Philip Schaff and Henry Wace (Grand Rapids, MI: Eerdman's Publishing Company, 1983), 92.

10. Ibid.

Him, who bruised the heads of the dragon."[11] We shouldn't think less of this because it is free, he concludes, but for that very reason honor the generous giver. Through this simple gesture we too can profess our faith, sanctify the events of our daily life and invoke the power of God.

The Sign of the Cross, as with many liturgical signs, conveys a wealth of meaning. It is the mark of those zealous for the holiness and glory of God and a sign of the power of God displayed in the cross of Christ. St. Cyril's description of the Sign of the Cross as a great preservative and weapon against the enemy is a wonderful example of how a sacramental sign makes present the reality it signifies. The Sign of the Cross truly enables us to "enter into the power of the blessing of Christ."[12]

The Sign of the Cross in the Sacraments

Where, how often, and by whom is the Sign of the Cross made during the Mass?

What is the meaning of each of these signs of the cross?

Silence

Another, somewhat different kind of liturgical sign is silence. In its *Constitution on the Sacred Liturgy*, the Second Vatican Council listed it as one of the elements of active participation: "To promote active participation, the people should be encouraged to take part by means of acclamations, responses, psalmody, antiphons, and songs, as well as by actions, gestures, and bearing. And at the proper times all should observe a reverent silence" (SC, 30). Liturgical silence is not merely an absence of words, nor is it simply a pause or interlude. "Rather, it is a stillness, a quieting of spirits, a taking time and leisure to hear, assimilate, and respond. . . . The dialogue between God and the community of faith taking place through the Holy Spirit requires intervals of silence, suited to the congregation, so that all can take to heart the word of God and respond to it in prayer" (IOM, 48). Note especially the language of relationship and encounter—hearing the word of God addressed to us, understanding it, and responding to the One who has addressed us. Silence, then, facilitates relationship with the Blessed

---

11. Ibid.

12. Ratzinger, *The Spirit of the Liturgy*, 184.

Trinity and becomes a means to greater communion with the Father through the Son under the action of the Holy Spirit.

The purpose of liturgical silence varies. During the Mass, for example, in the Penitential Rite and after the invitation to pray before the Collect, it provides an opportunity for personal recollection. Following the readings or the Homily it creates a space for meditation on the proclaimed word. Silence after Communion is a time for prayer and praise. "This, in all truth, is the moment for an interior conversation with the Lord who has given himself to us, for that essential 'communicating' . . . without which the external reception of the Sacrament becomes mere ritual and therefore unfruitful."[13] St. Teresa of Avila urged her nuns to spend time in prayer after receiving Communion: "Be with Him willingly; don't lose so good an occasion for conversing with Him as is the hour after having received Communion. . . . This, then, is a good time for our Master to teach us, and for us to listen to Him, kiss His feet because He wanted to teach us, and beg Him not to leave." "Why doubt," she asked, "if we have faith, that miracles will be worked while He is within us and that He will give what we ask of Him, since He is in our House? His Majesty is not accustomed to paying poorly for His lodging if the hospitality is good" (*Way of Perfection*, 34). Silence at different moments in the liturgy develops our docility to the Holy Spirit.

Silence during the liturgy can be challenging, even uncomfortable. "Ours is not an age which fosters recollection; at times one has the impression that people are afraid of detaching themselves, even for a moment, from the mass media" (VD, 66). This calls for a special catechesis on the meaning of silence in the liturgy in order to rediscover "a sense of recollection and inner repose. Only in silence can the word of God find a home in us, as it did in Mary, woman of the word and, inseparably, woman of silence. Our liturgies must facilitate this attitude of authentic listening" (VD, 66). In the words of the great Spanish doctor Saint John of the Cross, "The Father spoke one Word, which was his Son, and this Word he speaks always in eternal silence, and in silence must it be heard by the soul."[14]

---

13. Ibid., 210.

14. John of the Cross, *The Collected Works of St. John of the Cross*, trans. Kieran Kavanaugh, OCD, and Otilio Rodriguez, OCD (Washington, DC: ICS Publications, 1991), 92.

Silence

The Church suggests silence during the Mass at seven different points:

1. Prior to the beginning of Mass (GIRM, 45)

2. Prior to the Penitential Act (GIRM, 54)

3. After the invitation to pray (before the Collect) (GIRM, 54)

4. Before the Liturgy of the Word begins (GIRM, 56)

5. After the first and second readings (GIRM, 56)

6. After the homily (GIRM, 56)

7. After communion

At which of these points is silence most meaningful for you?

Movement

Movement is another important liturgical sign. The prescribed movements of the ministers and people manifest important aspects of the sacramental reality that is being celebrated. A good example is the Sacrament of Baptism. One of the fruits of Baptism is that the recipient is incorporated into the Church of Christ. This sacramental reality is manifested through the movements and stations of the rite, what Douglas Martis calls the "geography" of the sacrament. It typically begins at the entrance of the church signifying that one is asking for membership in the Church. Here all are welcomed, the parents are questioned, the child is signed on the forehead, and the liturgy of the word is celebrated in the nave, followed by the prayer of exorcism and the prebaptismal anointing. At the entrance to the church these introductory rites prepare one for membership in the Church.

Following the anointing with the oil of catechumens, the recipient goes to the baptismal font for the celebration of the sacrament: the blessing of the baptism water, renunciation of sin and profession of faith, baptism, clothing with the white garment, presentation of the lighted candle, and the prayer over the ears and mouth. Through these rites the child's sins are forgiven, he or she is made a child of God, a temple of the Holy Spirit, and a member of Christ's Church. This sacramental reality is next signified by a procession to the altar, which also manifests the fact that baptism is oriented to Eucharistic communion. Here the assembly prays the Lord's Prayer, receives a blessing from the celebrant, and is dismissed. The Rite of Baptism thus takes place at three distinct stations—the entrance of the church, the baptismal font, and the altar—which physically manifest the spiritual reality being enacted.

Movement is also an important part of the Eucharist. The Mass includes four separate processions: the entrance procession, the procession with the Book of the Gospels, the procession with the gifts, and the communion procession. With the exception of the Gospel procession, all the processions begin in the nave and move to the sanctuary. This reflects the symbolism of the church building. The sanctuary is the fulfillment of the Old Testament holy of holies as well as an image of the heavenly Jerusalem, the dwelling place of God. The nave is the dwelling of the people of God. "In this perspective, procession represents the pilgrimage of the people of God to its heavenly homeland; it represents the union of God and man, begun now in grace, and progressing toward its perfection in glory."[15]

Let's look more closely at one of these processions, the procession with the gifts of bread, wine, and money that follows the Prayers of the Faithful. It normally begins in the nave and moves to the sanctuary where the gifts are received by the priest. This procession manifests a rich symbolism. It expresses the congregation's participation in the Eucharist, an aspect that "is best expressed if the procession passes right through their midst" (IOM, 105). It also manifests "the humble and contrite heart, the dispossession of self that is necessary for making the true offering, which the Lord Jesus gave his people to make for him. The procession with the gifts expresses also our eager willingness to enter into the 'holy exchange' with God: 'accept the offerings you have given us, that we in turn may receive the gift of yourself [Prayer over the Offerings]'" (IOM, 105).

This procession is also a form of intercession for the world, as Pope Benedict XVI explains: "This humble and simple gesture is actually very significant: in the bread and wine that we bring to the altar, all creation is taken up by Christ the Redeemer to be transformed and

---

15. John Mary Burns, "The Procession of the *Ordo Missae*: Liturgical Structure and Theological Meaning," *Antiphon* 13, no. 2 (2009): 162.

presented to the Father. In this way we also bring to the altar all the pain and suffering of the world, in the certainty that everything has value in God's eyes" (SacCar, 47). So what can appear as a strictly functional action is in fact a movement of profound spiritual meaning and power. It expresses the participation of the assembly in the Mass, the humility and contrition of the people of God, their willingness to offer themselves, and their intercession for the whole world.

Movement then is one of the ways that the liturgy engages the whole person. It also reveals the sacramentality of the church building and effects the participation of the faithful in the liturgy. It reminds us that here we are "aliens and sojourners" (1 Pt 2:11) whose "citizenship is in heaven" (Phil 3:20) toward which we journey as God's "pilgrim Church on earth" (Eucharistic Prayer III). Finally, liturgical movement helps form in us the proper dispositions for fruitful participation in sacramental celebrations.

Incense

The liturgy also makes use of different kinds of material signs, for example, water, oil, and bread. Incense is one of the material signs used in a number of liturgical celebrations. It is recommended for more solemn celebrations of the Eucharist, during exposition and benediction of the Blessed Sacrament, in the rite of dedication of a church and altar, at solemn celebrations of Morning Prayer and Evening Prayer, funerals, and "in any procession of some solemnity" (CB, 88). Incense is another kind of liturgical language, another way that the liturgy engages the whole person, for it appeals to our senses of sight and smell. For this reason, the Church encourages its use "in amounts sufficient to be seen and smelled" (IOM, 58).

As a liturgical sign, incense is rich in meanings. First and foremost, it is a sign of prayer. This meaning is rooted in the Old and New Testaments. The psalmist begged God, "Let my prayer be incense before you" (Ps 141:2). St. John saw it used in the heavenly liturgy: "Another angel came and stood at the altar, holding a golden censer. He was given a great quantity of incense to offer, along with the prayers of all the holy ones, on the gold altar that was before the throne" (Rev 8:3). It also symbolizes the Church's gifts rising to the Father. During the Mass, the gifts on the altar as well as the cross and altar are incensed "so as to signify the Church's offering and prayer rising like incense in the sight of God" (GIRM, 75). In addition, incense is a sign of the dignity of the ordained ministry as well as the priesthood of the baptized: "the Priest, because of his sacred ministry, and the people, by reason of their baptismal dignity, may be incensed by the Deacon or by another minister" (GIRM, 75). Incense is also an expression of reverence, "a sign of respect and honor" (IOM, 58) before Christ. In addition, it recalls the pillar of cloud (Ex 13:21) by which God led Israel in the wilderness, the cloud itself symbolizing "God's glory and presence in the midst of the Israelites" (IOM, 58). In this way it "suggests both the otherness of the transcendent God and . . . can contribute powerfully to a sense of mystery" (IOM, 58).

The use of incense in the liturgy expresses many meanings. It signifies the prayers and gifts of the assembly rising up to God. It acknowledges Christ present as Head (in the ordained minister) and Body (all the baptized). It is a sign of the dignity of the ordained ministers and the priesthood of the baptized who together celebrate the liturgy as Christ Head and Body. It engages yet another of our senses, contributing to the participation of the whole person. Finally, it conveys reverence for Christ and the transcendent otherness of God present in the midst of his people, enriching the solemnity and mystery of the liturgy.

Incense

During the Mass, incense can be used at five points: the entrance procession, the introductory rites, the proclamation of the Gospel, the preparation of the gifts, and the elevation of the sacred species following the consecration.

What is the significance of incense at each of these points?

Liturgical Colors

The last liturgical sign we will examine is color. Pope Innocent III (1198–1216) first determined specific colors for specific days, and his choices are essentially those still in force today: white, red, green, and black. However, it wasn't until the Missal of 1570 that an obligatory liturgical color scheme first appeared. The approved liturgical colors in the United States are white, red, green, violet or purple, black, and rose (GIRM, 346). Gold and silver are approved for use in the United States "on more solemn occasions" (GIRM, 346). In the liturgy, colors contribute to the expression of "the specific character of the mysteries of faith to be celebrated" (GIRM, 345), which we will now consider.

White is a symbol of God, who dwells in unapproachable light (1 Tm 6:16) and of Christ, "the light of the world" (Jn 8:12). Therefore, it is used during Christmas Time, Easter Time, the Solemnity of the Most Holy Trinity, and celebrations of the Lord (except for the Passion). It is also a sign of purity, so it is also used for celebrations of the Blessed Virgin Mary, of the Holy Angels, and of the Saints who were not martyrs. It is also used on a few other liturgical celebrations such as the Solemnity of All Saints (November 1) and the feast of the Conversion of St. Paul (January 25).[16] Finally, white is a sign of joy, and so it is used in processions with the Blessed Sacrament, and in the sacraments of Baptism, Confirmation (if not red), Anointing of the Sick, and Viaticum. The joy of the angels at the birth of Christ, his resurrection victory over sin and death, the radiance of the Blessed Trinity, and the purity and radiance of the saints all find liturgical expression in the color white.

Like the color white, the color red also signifies diverse aspects of the faith. It is the color of fire, which is one of the biblical images of the Holy Spirit (Acts 2:3), so it is used on Pentecost Sunday and in the celebration of the sacrament of Confirmation within the Mass. As the color of blood, it signifies the suffering of the Lord and the saints, so it is also used on Palm Sunday, Good Friday, celebrations of the Lord's Passion, and on the celebrations of saints who were martyred. The color red is a sign to us of Christ's suffering with us and for us, of the faithful and courageous testimony of the martyrs, and of "the Gift that contains all gifts, the Holy Spirit" (CCC, 1082).

Green, the color of springtime, new growth, and hope, is used in Ordinary Time, especially "in the ordinary Sundays of the year, which are commemorations of the great Sunday of the Resurrection, when hope once again returned to the world."[17] The color violet or purple is a sign of sorrow, mourning, penance, and repentance. Thus, it is used in Advent and Lent, as well as in the sacrament of Penance. Rose, a sign of

---

16. Liturgical celebrations are categorized according to their importance. First in importance are solemnities, such as the Immaculate Conception of the Blessed Virgin Mary (December 8), which begin on the evening of the preceding day. Next in importance are feasts, such as the Feast of the Transfiguration (August 6). Third in rank are memorials, which are either obligatory or optional.

17. Virgil Michel, OSB, *The Liturgy of the Church* (New York: MacMillan, 1937), 77.

subdued joy, is used during the penitential seasons of Advent (on *Gaudete* Sunday, the Third Sunday of Advent) and Lent (on *Laetare* Sunday, the Fourth Sunday of Lent). Although white is most commonly worn at funerals, violet and black, a symbol today of mourning and death, are also permitted.

In addition to expressing the specific character of the liturgical mysteries, liturgical colors also give "a sense of Christian life's passage through the course of the liturgical year" (GIRM, 345). "In the liturgical year the various aspects of the one Paschal mystery unfold" (CCC, 1171). In the course of the liturgical year the Church recalls "the mysteries of redemption . . . [and] opens to the faithful the riches of the Lord's powers and merits, so that these are in some way made present in every age in order that the faithful may lay hold on them and be filled with saving grace" (SC, 102). However, the liturgical year, which begins with Advent, does not unfold in a strictly chronological order (if it did, Easter would be celebrated at the end of the year rather than in the middle). Rather, taking

the Easter Triduum as its source of light, the new age of the Resurrection fills the whole liturgical year with its brilliance. Gradually, on either side of this source, the year is transfigured by the liturgy. It really is a 'year of the Lord's favor.' The economy of salvation is at work within the framework of time, but since its fulfillment in the Passover of Jesus and the outpouring of the Holy Spirit, the culmination of history is anticipated 'as a foretaste,' and the kingdom of God enters into our time" (CCC, 1168).

This unfolding of time now transfigured by the "new age of the Resurrection" finds expression in the liturgical use of color. The brilliance of the Resurrection is signified by the use of white, gold, or silver throughout the season of Easter. The use of violet or purple in the forty days leading up to the Triduum assists us in preparing for the great event through sorrow, contrition, and penance. The green of Ordinary Time that precedes Lent and follows Easter is a sign of hope and faith as the events of our Lord's life, which find their definitive power and fulfillment in the age of the Resurrection and the riches of our Lord's powers and merits, are made liturgically present. Finally, the overflowing radiance of the Triduum reaches back to the penitential and expectant character of Advent, expressed through the use of violet/purple vestments, while also reaching forward to the radiant culmination of the liturgical year, the Solemnity of Christ the King, symbolized by white, silver, or gold. In this way we see how the liturgical colors visually express our pilgrim journey toward our heavenly homeland.

Liturgical colors combine with the other liturgical signs to make present the various aspects of the one Paschal Mystery. They characterize the central mystery of our faith, the Paschal Mystery. Within the major seasons of the liturgical year—Advent, Christmas, Ordinary Time, Lent, and Easter—are expressed the individual events and mysteries of the life of Christ and the saints. In the liturgy, colors contribute to the expression of "the specific character of the mysteries of faith to be celebrated" (GIRM, 345), aiding us in entering into the liturgy with our whole being.

Liturgical Color

What is the liturgical color for each of the following celebrations?

The Assumption (August 15)

Triumph of the Cross (September 14)

The Lord's Supper (Holy Thursday)

Christ the King (Last Sunday in Ordinary Time)

The Sacred Heart (Friday following the Second Sunday after Pentecost)

THE ESSENTIAL RITE

For centuries the Church, using the language of medieval Scholastic theology, has identified two elements as necessary for the celebration of each sacrament, the *matter* and the *form*. The matter is the required visible, material element (e.g., water for Baptism, grape wine and unleavened wheat bread for the Eucharist), and the form is the prayer that accompanies and explains the matter. In the case of the Sacrament of Penance and Reconciliation the matter "is not so straightforward because there is no immediately visible element upon which the creative word [the form] can confer a salvific meaning."[18] The Church

---

18. Paul Haffner, *The Sacramental Mystery*, rev. ed. (Herefordshire, UK: Gracewing, 2007), 152.

considers the acts of the penitent—confession, contrition, and satisfaction—the quasi-matter (quasi meaning "as it were"[19]) of the sacrament. Similarly, the Sacrament of Marriage lacks a visible element that constitutes the matter: "the matter is the mutual self-giving of the spouses, and the form is the mutual acceptance of this self-giving."[20] As these examples illustrate, the terms matter and form more clearly describe the key elements of some sacraments than of others.

The *Catechism of the Catholic Church* does not use the scholastic language of *matter* and *form*, referring instead to the "essential rite." For example, the essential rite for Baptism is the triple immersion in the baptismal water, or the triple pouring of water—the matter, along with the words, "N., I baptize you in the name of the Father, and of the Son, and of the Holy Spirit"—the form (CCC, 1239–1240). If the "essential rite" is changed or omitted, the sacrament is invalid; in other words, it did not take place. When discussing the individual sacraments, we will use the language of the *Catechism*, the essential rite, rather than the scholastic language of *matter* and *form*.

HARMONY OF SIGNS

While the individual liturgical signs constitute a complex liturgical language that appeals to different senses and engages the whole person, they also combine in a harmonious way to make present in all of its richness the one Paschal Mystery of Christ. For this reason, the *Catechism* speaks of "the harmony of signs" (1158), the way that words and silence, movement and gesture, song and music, sight and smell, combine to make present in its fullness the Paschal Mystery.

The *Catechism* cites the contemplation of sacred icons as an example of this harmony of signs: "the contemplation of sacred icons, united with meditation on the Word of God and the singing of liturgical hymns, enters into the harmony of the signs of celebration so that the mystery celebrated is imprinted in the heart's memory and is then expressed in the new life of the faithful" (CCC, 1162). Here we see how three liturgical signs—sacred images, Sacred Scripture, and sacred music—together make present a specific event ("the mystery celebrated") from the life of our Lord (e.g., the Nativity, the Transfiguration, or the

---

19. Ibid., 153.
20. Ibid., 243–244.

Resurrection) or the Blessed Virgin Mary (e.g., the Annunciation, the Visitation, or the Crucifixion) that can transform the life of the faithful.

While we have considered examples of the different kinds of signs that comprise the language of the liturgy, these elements do not occur in isolation. Rather, they combine in distinct but complementary ways to make present the one Paschal Mystery of Christ through which the Father draws us into the Trinitarian life of love through his beloved Son in the Holy Spirit. The more we can understand and appreciate the meaning and harmony of the different signs, the more effectively are we able to participate fully, actively, and consciously in the liturgy for our sanctification and the glory of God.

Harmony of Signs

An example of this harmony of signs that is familiar to all Catholics is the Communion Rite of the Mass. Receiving the Body and Blood of the Lord "in a paschal meal is the culmination of the Eucharist" (IOM, 125). The Communion Rite is composed of the following elements: The Lord's Prayer, the Rite of Peace, the Fraction Rite, Communion (including procession), the Communion Chant, and the Prayer after Communion. While each element is rich in meaning, "in the context of the whole celebration they constitute together a transition from one high point, the Eucharistic Prayer, to another, the sharing in Holy Communion" (IOM, 125).

1. Which of the liturgical signs and symbols discussed in chapters 1 and 2 are present in the Communion Rite? Consider such things as words, silence, movement, color, posture, images, and song.

2. How do these different liturgical signs contribute to the effectiveness of this part of the Mass?

3. What might hinder or disrupt the harmony of signs?

CONCLUSION

In one of his letters on Holy Thursday, St. John Paul II encouraged pastors to instruct the faithful on the meaning of the signs and symbols of the liturgy "by which the faithful are helped to understand the meaning of the liturgy's words and actions, to pass from its signs to the mystery which they contain, and to enter into that mystery in every aspect of their lives" (MND, 17). This exhortation eloquently summarizes the dynamic nature of the language of the liturgy. The signs and symbols of the liturgy "contain" the mystery that they signify. However, it is only when we understand the liturgical signs and symbols that we are able "to pass from its signs to the mystery they contain," for "when minds are enlightened and hearts are enkindled, signs begin to 'speak'" (MND, 14). This is the essence of full, active, and conscious participation in the liturgy, passing from its visible signs to an encounter with the Blessed Trinity and the power of the Paschal Mystery which they contain and make present.

Chapter 3

From Sign to Mystery: Mystagogical Catechesis

As we have seen in the preceding chapters, through the faith of the Church and the power of the Holy Spirit, God communicates the fruits of Christ's Paschal Mystery to us by means of a rich and varied liturgical language that engages the whole person. The challenge for us today is mastering the language of the liturgy, a task that "is particularly important in a highly technological age like our own, which risks losing the ability to appreciate signs and symbols" (SacCar, 64). It is the task of liturgical catechists to "initiate people into the mystery of Christ by proceeding from the visible to the invisible, from the sign to the thing signified, from the 'sacraments' to the 'mysteries'" (CCC, 1075). This type of catechesis is called *mystagogy*, from the Greek word for the person who led an initiate into a mystery. Its goal is to lead people from the signs to the spiritual realities they signify.

St. John Paul II encouraged this kind of catechesis. "Pastors should be committed to that *'mystagogical' catechesis* so dear to the Fathers of the Church, by which the faithful are helped to understand the meaning of the liturgy's words and actions, to pass from its signs to the mystery which they contain, and to enter into that mystery in every aspect of their lives" (MND, 17). He affirms the theme of the previous chapter: liturgical signs contain the mystery they signify. Pope Francis, speaking specifically of the sacraments of initiation, has also encouraged a mystagogical approach to catechesis that involves the whole community and opens up the meaning of liturgical signs. Such an approach, writes Pope Francis, should be part of "a broader growth process and the integration of every dimension of the person within a communal journey of hearing and response" (EG, 166). Understanding the words and actions of the liturgy enables us to pass from the outward signs and actions of the liturgy to the spiritual reality and power they contain. The sacraments have the power to utterly transform every aspect of our lives.

Mystagogical catechesis is a part of the Church's Tradition, a method of catechesis "so dear to the Fathers of the Church" (MND, 17).

In the first centuries of the Church, following the reception of the sacraments of initiation—Baptism, a post-baptismal anointing which we know as Confirmation, and first Eucharist—the new Christians were given a detailed catechesis explaining the meaning of the sacraments and the significance of the words and actions of the rite they had just received. The purpose of mystagogical catechesis was not to prepare people to receive the sacraments, but rather to help them understand more deeply the sacraments they had just received. The fourth century was the golden age of mystagogical catechesis. From this period we have important mystagogical texts from such illustrious Church Fathers as St. Cyril of Jerusalem (d. 386), St. Ambrose (d. 397), and St. John Chrysostom (d. 407). The writings of the Church Fathers continue to instruct us about the meaning of the sacraments and constitute an important source for our exploration of the sacraments.

Pope Benedict XVI expanded St. John Paul II's emphasis on catechesis that leads people into the mystery. In *Sacrament of Charity*, he proposed a model of mystagogical catechesis consisting of three elements.

1. *"It interprets the rites in the light of the events of our salvation,* in accordance with the Church's living tradition. . . . From the beginning, the Christian community has interpreted the events of Jesus' life, and the Paschal Mystery in particular, in relation to the entire history of the Old Testament."
2. Mystagogical catechesis explains *"the meaning of the signs* contained in the rites."
3. It should emphasize "the *significance of the rites for the Christian life* in all its dimensions—work and responsibility, thoughts and emotions, activity and repose." Ultimately, this kind of catechesis should lead to "an awareness that one's life is being progressively transformed by the holy mysteries being celebrated" (SacCar, 64).

OLD TESTAMENT ROOTS

The first part of a mystagogical catechesis is to explain the rites in the light of its Old Testament roots. The sacraments of the Church are prefigured by the Old Testament persons (Adam, Joseph, Isaac, and David, for example, prefigured in different ways the person and work of Christ) and events, such as anointing, the consecration of kings and priests, sacrifices, the laying on of hands, and above all the Passover. "The Church sees in these signs a prefiguring of the sacraments of the New Covenant" (CCC, 1150). The persons and events of the Old Testament point to the mysteries of Christ and reveal different aspects of his Paschal Mystery, "for he himself is the meaning of all of these signs" (CCC, 1151). There are three readily available sources that reveal the Old Testament roots of each sacrament:

> The rite itself
> The biblical readings proscribed in the rite for each sacrament
> *The Catechism of the Catholic Church*

The Rite Itself

The rite itself is always the best starting point, for these are the words we hear and say, the gestures and postures we adopt, and the signs and symbols that engage us, and that lead us deeper into the mystery of the sacrament. As mentioned earlier, the liturgy is one of the primary ways that the Church has passed on the faith entrusted to her by the Lord. Christ has entrusted to the Church the responsibility of passing "on the faith in its integrity so that the 'rule of prayer' (*lex orandi*) of the Church may correspond to the 'rule of faith' (*lex credendi*)" (VL, 27). The terms "rule of prayer" (*lex orandi*) and "rule of faith" (*lex credendi*) refer to a principle that dates back to Prosper of Aquitaine (fifth century). The *Catechism of the Catholic Church* explains this principle: "The law of prayer is the law of faith: the Church believes as she prays. Liturgy is a constitutive element of the holy and living Tradition" (1124). Another Church Father, St. Irenaeus (late second century), expressed this principle with respect to the Mass: "Our way of thinking is attuned to the Eucharist, and the Eucharist in turn confirms our way of thinking" (CCC, 1327). From the earliest days the Church has understood the inseparable relationship between her worship and her faith, and for this reason the sacramental rite is always the best starting point for understanding the meaning of the sacrament itself.

An excellent example of this is Eucharistic Prayer I (the Roman Canon) from the Mass. Following the consecration, there is a prayer asking God to accept "these offerings . . . as once you were pleased to accept the gifts of your servant Abel the just, the sacrifice of Abraham, our father in faith, and the offering of your high priest Melchizedek." Let us look closely at the last example, "the offering of your high priest

Melchizedek." This event is recounted in Genesis 14:17–20. Melchizedek, the king of Salem, meets Abraham as he is returning victorious from battle. Melchizedek is described as a priest, and he brings bread and wine and blesses Abraham, who then gives Melchizedek a tenth of the spoils. St. Cyprian (d. 258) described Melchizedek as "a type of Christ" (an identification that is extensively developed in the Letter to the Hebrews). Cyprian emphasizes Melchizedek's offering of bread and wine and his blessing of Abraham. "For who is more a priest of the most high God," he asks, "than our Lord Jesus Christ, who offered sacrifice to God the Father and offered the very same thing that Melchizedek had offered, bread and wine, that is, actually, his body and blood?"[1]

Prefigurement of the Eucharist in the Old Testament

Read the accounts of "the gifts of Abel" (Gn 4:1–16) and "the sacrifice of Abraham" (Gn 22:1–19). In what ways do these reveal different aspects of the Eucharist?

The Biblical Readings for Each Sacrament

Each sacrament includes suggested Old Testament readings, responsorial psalms, passages from the New Testament epistles, and appropriate selections from the Gospels, all chosen to highlight different aspects of the sacrament being celebrated. For example, one of the Old Testament options for the Sacrament of Penance and Reconciliation is 2 Samuel 12:1–9, 13. In this passage the prophet Nathan confronts David concerning his affair with Bathsheba and arranging the death of Uriah her husband. David acknowledges his sinful actions, and Nathan replies that God has forgiven his sin. This Old Testament account prefigures several important aspects of the sacrament of Penance: grave sin, contrition, and the announcement of forgiveness by God's representative.

Catechism of the Catholic Church

A third source for exploring the Old Testament roots of each sacrament is the *Catechism of the Catholic Church*. As an example, let's look at the Sacrament of Confirmation. The *Catechism* finds the Old Testament

---

1. Mark Sheridan, ed., *Genesis 12–50,* Ancient Christian Commentary on Scripture (Downers Grove, IL: InterVaristy Press, 2002), 26.

roots of this sacrament in the prophetic announcement of the Spirit-anointed Messiah in Isaiah 11:2: "And the spirit of the LORD shall rest upon him: a spirit of wisdom and of understanding, a spirit of counsel and of strength, a spirit of knowledge and of fear of the LORD" (CCC, 1286).[2] The descent of the Spirit upon Jesus at his baptism is the sign that he is the fulfillment of Isaiah's prophecy. The prophecies of two other Old Testament figures, Ezekiel (36:25–27) and Joel (3:1–2), affirm that the Spirit was to be given "to the *whole messianic people*" (CCC, 1287). "From that time on the apostles, in fulfillment of Christ's will, imparted to the newly baptized by the laying on of hands the gift of the Spirit that completes the grace of Baptism" (CCC, 1288).

Let's take a more detailed look at an example of the Old Testament roots of Baptism as found in the rite itself in the blessing of the baptismal waters. The prayer begins as follows (I have included the rubric, which is an important sacramental sign [described in chapter 1]).

> *With hands outstretched he says:*
> O God, who by invisible power
> accomplish a wondrous effect
> through sacramental signs
> and who in many ways have prepared water, your creation,
> to show forth the grace of Baptism . . . (RM, Easter Vigil,
> Blessing of Baptismal Water)

This opening stanza concisely expresses the sacramental principle: God communicates the power and fruits of the Paschal Mystery to us through sacramental signs to "accomplish a wondrous effect." As we discussed in chapter 2, God mediates his presence to us through signs and symbols taken from human culture, the Old Testament, and, in the case of Baptism, creation itself—water. This stanza further explains that God has used water "in many ways" to express the grace of Baptism. The succeeding stanzas will give three different Old Testament examples of how God prepared water "to show forth the grace of Baptism." Each stanza cites one Old Testament example and explains how it reveals a specific aspect of Baptism.

The first Old Testament event cited in this prayer is the account of creation in Genesis 1.

---

2. The earliest reference we have to this passage as included in the prayer that accompanies the imposition of hands is St. Ambrose (d. 397).

> O God, whose Spirit
> in the first moments of the world's creation
> hovered over the waters,
> so that the very substance of water
> would even then take to itself the power to sanctify . . .
> (RM, Easter Vigil, Blessing of Baptismal Water)

The reference here is to Genesis 1:2: "the Spirit of God was moving over the face of the waters" (Revised Standard Version Catholic Edition). The Spirit moving over the waters is seen as a sort of primordial epiclesis (see chapter 1) in which the Spirit imparts to water the power to sanctify. St. Jerome (d. 420) saw in this passage a prefigurement of Baptism: "already at that time baptism was being foreshadowed."[3] Tertullian (d. ca. 220), in his interpretation of this passage from Genesis, specifically emphasized the power of water to sanctify: "The Holy One was carried over that which was holy, or, rather, over that which could receive holiness from Him Who was carried. It is thus that the nature of water, sanctified by the Spirit, received the capability of itself becoming sanctifying. This is why all waters, by reason of their ancient original prerogative, may obtain the sacrament of sanctification [Baptism] by the invocation of God."[4] Through the power of the Spirit, material substances such as water can receive the power to convey holiness.

The prayer next invokes the flood as described in Genesis 6 and 7.

> O God, who by the outpouring of the flood
> foreshadowed regeneration,
> so that from the mystery of one and the same element of water
> would come an end to vice and a beginning of virtue . . .
> (RM, Easter Vigil, Blessing of Baptismal Water)

God, grieved by the wickedness of mankind, sent a flood to blot out all vice while preserving life through Noah, who was righteous and blameless (Gn 6:9). St. Augustine saw in the flood a prefigurement of Baptism: "Who does not know, indeed, that in other times the earth was purified from its stains by the Flood. And that the mystery of holy Baptism, by which all the sins of man were cleansed by the water, was

---

3. Andrew Louth, ed., *Genesis 1–11*, Ancient Christian Commentary on Scripture (Downers Grove, IL: InterVarsity Academic Press, 2001), 6.

4. Jean Daniélou, SJ, *The Bible and the Liturgy* (Notre Dame, IN: University of Notre Dame Press, 1956), 72–73.

preached already beforehand?"[5] Through Baptism our sins are forgiven and the gift of the Spirit enables us to live a life of holiness for God.

The final Old Testament reference in the prayer of blessing is Israel's exodus from Egypt recounted in Exodus 14.

> O God, who caused the children of Abraham
> to pass dry-shod through the Red Sea,
> so that the chosen people
> set free from slavery to Pharaoh,
> would prefigure the people of the baptized . . . (RBC)

St. Paul, in his First Letter to the Corinthians, interpreted the exodus from Egypt as a type of Baptism: "all passed through the sea, and all of them were baptized into Moses in the cloud and in the sea" (10:1–2). St. Basil the Great developed this interpretation: "The sea is the figure of Baptism, since it delivered the people from Pharaoh, as Baptism from the tyranny of the devil. The sea killed the enemy; so in Baptism, our enmity to God is destroyed. The people came out of the sea whole and safe; we also come out of the water as living men from among the dead."[6] St. Gregory of Nyssa also saw in the Exodus a figure of Baptism: "when the people approach the water of rebirth as they flee from Egypt, which is sin, they themselves are freed and saved, but the devil and his aids, the spirits of wickedness, are destroyed."[7] Baptism, then, frees us from slavery to sin just as the Exodus freed the chosen people from slavery to Pharaoh.

These three Old Testament passages reveal important aspects of the sacrament of Baptism. From creation we learn that the baptismal waters receive from the Spirit the power to sanctify believers. Baptism, like the Flood, brings an end to the reign of sin and the beginning of holiness. Finally, Baptism, like the Exodus, frees us from slavery to sin and brings us into "the glorious freedom of the children of God" (Rom 8:21).

---

5. Ibid., 279.
6. Ibid., 90.
7. Ibid.

Mystagogical Catechesis: Meaning of the Signs

An effective mystagogical catechesis *explains the meaning of the different signs contained in the rites*. The liturgical signs are essential because they are "bearers of the saving and sanctifying action of Christ" (CCC, 1189). Furthermore, we need to understand these signs, because only when we understand them are we able to pass from the signs to the mystery they contain. The sacraments differ in their complexity and in the number and variety of the signs and symbols. The Mass, for example, employs a greater number of liturgical signs than the Sacrament of Penance and Reconciliation. In addition, while many signs are common to many if not all of the sacraments (see again chapter 2), each sacrament has some elements that are unique to that sacrament.

For example, let's look at a couple of signs that comprise the Sacrament of the Anointing of the Sick when celebrated in a hospital or institution. The outline of this rite is as follows: Introductory Rites (Greeting and Instruction), Liturgy of Anointing (Laying On of Hands, Anointing, the Lord's Prayer, Prayer after Anointing), and Concluding Rite (Blessing). Here we will consider the sign of the oil of the sick, the prayer of blessing over the oil, and the imposition of hands.

Anointing with oil is a rich sign of healing. The Old Testament prophet Isaiah laments the wounds of sinful Israel that are not "eased with salve" (1:6). The Good Samaritan of Luke's Gospel dressed the wounds of his injured neighbor with oil and wine (Lk 10:34). In Mark's account of the Gospel, Christ sent the Twelve to continue his healing ministry, and they "anointed with oil many who were sick and cured them" (6:13). The Letter of James confirms that the early Church continued this healing ministry: "Is anyone among you sick? He should summon the presbyters of the church, and they should pray over him and anoint him with oil in the name of the Lord" (5:14). In his commentary on this verse, Hilary of Arles says that "the grace of mercy is symbolized by oil."[8] Oil as a sign of healing is an excellent example of how the Sacred Scriptures help us understand the meaning of sacramental signs.

The *Catechism* and the rite itself offer additional meanings. The *Catechism* says that anointing the sick with oil "expresses healing and

---

8. Gerald Bray, ed., *James, 1–2 Peter, 1–3 John, Jude*, Ancient Christian Commentary on Scripture (Downers Grove, IL: InterVarsity Academic Press, 2000), 60.

comfort" (1294). According to *Pastoral Care of the Sick* (the official ritual book for the anointing of the sick), anointing the sick with oil signifies not only healing but also "strengthening, and the presence of the Spirit" (PCS, 107). "The Church's use of oil for healing," it concludes, "is closely related to its remedial use in soothing and comforting the sick and in restoring the tired and the weak. Thus the sick person is strengthened to fight against the physically and spiritually debilitating effects of illness" (PCS, 107).

The prayer of blessing over the oil deepens our understanding of this sacramental sign and expresses its power.

> God of all consolation,
> you chose and sent your Son to heal the world.
> Graciously listen to our prayer of faith:
> send the power of your Holy Spirit, the Consoler,
> into this precious oil, this soothing ointment,
> this rich gift, this fruit of the earth.
> Bless this oil ✚ and sanctify it for our use.
> Make this oil a remedy for all who are anointed with it;
> heal them in body, in soul, and in spirit,
> and deliver them from every affliction. (PCS, 123)

This prayer begins by invoking the Holy Spirit upon the oil: "send the power of your Holy Spirit, the Consoler, into this precious oil, this soothing ointment, this rich gift, this fruit of the earth." This epiclesis acknowledges the oil as a rich gift and fruit of God's creation and imbues the oil with the power of the Spirit. The sign of the cross is then made over the oil: "Bless this oil ✚ and sanctify it for our use." Finally, the prayer expresses the comprehensive healing for which the Church prays—healing in body, soul and spirit, and deliverance from every affliction. In summary, "the prayer of blessing the oil of the sick reminds us, furthermore, that the oil of anointing is the sacramental sign of the presence, power, and grace of the Holy Spirit" (PCS, 107).

In the celebration of the sacrament, the recipient is anointed on the forehead and the palms of both hands while the following words are said: "Through this holy anointing may the Lord in his love and mercy help you with the grace of the Holy Spirit. May the Lord who frees you from sin save you and raise you up." These words and actions are the essential signs of the sacrament. The effectiveness of this sacramental symbol is further enhanced by "a generous use of oil so that it will be seen and felt by the sick person as a sign of the Spirit's healing and strengthening presence. For the same reason, it is not desirable to wipe off the oil after the anointing" (PCS, 107). The simplicity of these sacramental signs belies the paschal power that they communicate.

The last sign from this sacrament that we will consider is the imposition of hands. Before the priest anoints the sick person, he silently imposes his hands on the head of the sick person. This gesture has several meanings. First, it indicates that the recipient is the particular object of the Church's prayer. Second, the imposition of hands is a sign of blessing, "as we pray that by the power of God's healing grace the sick person may be restored to health or at least strengthened in time of illness" (PCS, 106). Third, it is the sign of the invocation of the Holy Spirit, as "the Church prays for the coming of the Holy Spirit upon the sick person" (PCS, 106). Finally, it is the biblical gesture of healing, "and indeed Jesus' own usual manner of healing" (PCS, 106) (see for example Mk 5:23; 6:5; 8:25; 10:16; Lk 4:40; and 13:13): "all who had people sick with various diseases brought them to him. He laid his hands on each of them and cured them" (Lk 4:40). The imposition of hands and the anointing with blessed oil are rich symbols that express the salvific meaning of this sacrament.

SIGNIFICANCE OF THE RITES FOR CHRISTIAN LIFE

The third aspect of effective mystagogical catechesis brings "out the *significance of the rites for the Christian life* in all its dimensions—work and responsibility, thoughts and emotions, activity and repose. Part of the mystagogical process is to demonstrate how the mysteries celebrated in the rite are linked to the missionary responsibility of the faithful. The mature fruit of mystagogy is an awareness that one's life is being progressively transformed by the holy mysteries being celebrated" (SacCar, 64). The sacraments both invite and enable us to conform our lives to the image of Christ.

SACRAMENTAL GRACE

The sacraments have the power to transform our lives because they communicate God's grace to us. The *Catechism* defines grace as "the *free and undeserved help* that God gives us to respond to his call to become children of God, adoptive sons, partakers of the divine nature and of eternal life" (CCC, 1996). It is "a *participation in the life of God*" that "introduces us into the intimacy of Trinitarian life" (CCC, 1997). Grace is "the gift of the Spirit who justifies and sanctifies us," but it also includes gifts that are proper to each of the sacraments, which is our concern here (CCC, 2003). The gifts or graces that are specific to each sacrament are signified by the corresponding sacramental signs, because each liturgical sign "points to what it specifically signifies."[9] For example, the Eucharistic bread and wine are signs of the Body and Blood of Christ. Furthermore, "the sacraments are given to us humans for the 'different situations of our life,' and consequently they must contain different effects of grace."[10] Put another way, "the grace imparted by the sacraments renders God's love, presence and power available in the present moment, in a way that is specific to each sacrament."[11] Reconciliation, for example, effects "a new today in Christ after we fall."[12] Through the gifts specific to each sacrament, God bestows on us the love and power to deepen our participation in the life of the Trinity.

However, it is also true that the sacraments are not equally fruitful in everyone who receives them. While everyone at Mass may receive the Body and Blood of Christ, the fruitfulness of this sacramental communion will vary. This is because "the fruits of the sacraments also depend on the disposition of the one who receives them" (CCC, 1128). The most obvious example is when someone receives a sacrament in a state of mortal sin, but other dispositions such as indifference or a lack of faith can also limit the fruitfulness of sacramental grace. This was true during Jesus' earthly ministry. When he went to Nazareth, his hometown, the people "took offense at him. . . . And he did not work many mighty deeds there because of their lack of faith" (Mt 13:57–58). On the other hand, Jesus praised the Canaanite woman who asked him to heal her daughter: "'O woman, great is your faith! Let it be done for you as you wish.' And her daughter was healed from that hour" (Mt 15:28). There is an intimate and reciprocal relationship between the

---

9. Johann Auer, *A General Doctrine of the Sacraments and the Mystery of The Eucharist* (Washington, DC: The Catholic University of America Press, 1995), 49.

10. Ibid.

11. Paul Haffner, *The Sacramental Mystery*, rev. ed. (Herefordshire: Gracewing, 2007), 21.

12. Ibid., 22.

sacraments and faith: "They not only presuppose faith, but by words and objects they also nourish, strengthen, and express it. That is why they are called 'sacraments *of faith*'" (CCC, 1123). Through the sacraments God imparts his help and life to us, but we must prepare ourselves to receive them with faith and humility.

TRANSFORMATION OF LIFE

As an example of the transforming power of the sacraments, let us look at the Sacrament of Confirmation. In addition to the sacramental rite, the biblical readings, the Church Fathers, and the *Catechism*, there is a fifth source of information about each sacrament: the orations (prayers) for the ritual Mass for the celebration of each of the sacraments (with the exception of the Sacrament of Reconciliation). For example, the ritual Mass for the conferral of Confirmation has two sets of prayers for the Collect (opening prayer), the Prayer over the Gifts, and the Prayer after Communion. Let us now look at the second set of prayers (B) to see what they reveal about the meaning of Confirmation for the whole of one's life.

We shall begin with the opening prayer, known as the Collect since it "collects" the prayers of the gathered assembly and offers them to the Father.

> Graciously pour out your Holy Spirit upon us,
> we pray, O Lord,
> so that, walking in oneness of faith
> and strengthened by the power of his love,
> we may come to the measure of the full stature of Christ.[13]

This prayer reveals several transforming aspects of the sacrament of Confirmation. It begins by imploring the gift of the Spirit which is the essential grace of the sacrament: "Graciously pour out your Holy Spirit upon us." It then enumerates three lifelong fruits. The first is working for the unity of all believers: "walking in oneness of faith." Jesus prayed for this unity in his high priestly prayer recorded in John 17: "I pray not only for them, but also for those who will believe in me through their word, so that they may all be one, as you, Father, are in me and I in you, that they also may be in us, that the world may believe

---

13. *Roman Missal*, Ritual Mass for the Conferral of Confirmation, Collect B.

that you sent me" (Jn 17:20–21). The second fruit is being strengthened by God's love, which according to St. Paul's Letter to the Romans is a specific gift of the Spirit: "the love of God has been poured into our hearts through the holy Spirit that has been given to us" (Rom 5:5). The third fruit is being conformed to the image of Christ: "we may come to the measure of the full stature of Christ." This petition is taken from the Letter to the Ephesians in which St. Paul speaks of the "building up of the body Christ, until we all attain to the unity of faith and knowledge of the Son of God, to mature manhood, to the extent of the full stature of Christ" (4:12–13). This brief but rich prayer expresses both the personal and the ecclesial: through the gift of the Spirit the recipient is strengthened by Christ's love and progressively conformed to his image so as to work for the unity of all believers that they together may come to "the full stature of Christ."

The second prayer is the Prayer over the Gifts, offered in response to the congregation's petition that the Lord would accept the sacrifice at the priest's hands "for the praise and glory of his name, for our good, and the good of all his holy Church" (*Order of Mass*, 29):

> Accept graciously these your servants, O Lord,
> together with your Only Begotten Son,
> so that, signed with his Cross and with a spiritual anointing,
> they may constantly offer themselves to you
> in union with him
> and merit each day a greater outpouring of your Spirit. [14]

This prayer begins by making reference to the essential signs of the Sacrament of Confirmation: "signed with his Cross and with a spiritual anointing." It then speaks of two specific transformative fruits. The first is a continual offering of oneself to the Father in union with Christ. This is the character of filial love, to offer oneself to God for the sake of others. The second fruit is a continued outpouring of the Spirit, for God "does not ration his gift of the Spirit" (Jn 3:34). As with the Collect, we see here both a personal dimension—an ever-greater outpouring of the Spirit—and an ecclesial dimension—the filial offering of oneself with Christ for the Church and the world.

---

14. *Roman Missal*, Ritual Mass for the Conferral of Confirmation, Prayer over the Offerings B.

The final prayer is the Prayer after Communion. Since it is proclaimed following the reception of sacramental communion, this prayer focuses on the fruits that flow from the reception of the Body and Blood of the Lord.

> Instruct, O Lord, in the fullness of the Law
> those you have endowed with the gifts of your Spirit
> and nourished by the Body of your Only Begotten Son,
> that they may constantly show to the world
> the freedom of your adopted children
> and, by the holiness of their lives,
> exercise the prophetic mission of your people. [15]

This prayer begins by affirming the relationship between Confirmation—"those you have endowed with the gifts of your Spirit"—and the Eucharist—"and nourished by the Body of your Only Begotten Son."

The Eucharist contains "the entire spiritual wealth of the church, namely Christ himself our Pasch and our living bread, who gives life to humanity through his flesh," and so all of the sacraments "are bound up with the Eucharist and are directed towards it" (PO, 5). This is especially true of the sacraments of initiation: "It must never be forgotten that our reception of Baptism and Confirmation is ordered to the Eucharist" (SacCar, 17). Thus transformed, those confirmed become signs to the world of the freedom of the children of God. Finally, the holiness made possible by the gifts of the Spirit enable the confirmed to participate in the prophetic mission of the Church, for "the gifts of the Spirit are given for the building up of Christ's Body (1 Cor 12) and for ever greater witness to the Gospel in the world" (SacCar 17). Again we see both personal and ecclesial effects: personal holiness and freedom which make believers signs to the world and prophetic witnesses to the world, if we are aware of and act with the graces we have received.

These prayers for the Mass for the Conferral of Confirmation contain a rich theology of the transforming power of the Sacrament of Confirmation. They indicate the different ways that one's entire life is progressively transformed by the sacrament: strengthened by God's love, increasingly conformed to the image of Christ, filled more and more with the Spirit, and walking in holiness. This personal

---

15. *Roman Missal*, Ritual Mass for the Conferral of Confirmation, Prayer after Communion B.

transformation expresses itself through participation in the mission of the Church, the Body of Christ: working for the unity of all believers, offering oneself to God with Christ for others, becoming ever more transparent living signs to the world of freedom in Christ, and offering a prophetic witness to the world.

CONCLUSION

In its *Constitution on the Sacred Liturgy*, the Second Vatican Council put special emphasis on "full, conscious, and active participation in liturgical celebrations" by all the faithful (SC, 14). "In the reform and promotion of the liturgy, this full and active participation by all the people is *the aim to be considered before all else*" (SC, 14, italics added). The Council's vision of participation has two dimensions, interior and exterior. Interior participation requires "a good understanding of the rites and prayers" so all present are "conscious of what they are doing, with devotion and full involvement" (SC, 48). Exterior participation means participating "by means of acclamations, responses, psalmody, antiphons, and songs, as well as by actions, gestures, and bearing. And at the proper times all should observe a reverent silence" (SC, 30). It also means that those who have a role to perform, whether minister or layperson, "should do all of, but only, those parts" proper to their office (SC, 28). The Church urges this full, conscious, and active participation because "it is the primary and indispensable source from which the faithful are to derive the true Christian spirit" (SC, 14).

The method of mystagogical catechesis proposed by Pope Benedict XVI and illustrated in this chapter can facilitate the kind of interior and exterior participation envisioned by the Church. Looking at the Old Testament roots of a sacrament reveals the unity of God's revelation in word and deed, a revelation that finds its fulfillment in Christ. Understanding the meaning of the liturgical signs, which carry within them the saving power of Christ's Paschal Mystery, enables us to pass from the signs to the mysteries they contain and to encounter Christ, who is the meaning of all of the signs. This in turn opens us up to the transforming power of each sacrament so that we may know the love of Christ which surpasses knowledge and adore the one who "is able to accomplish far more than all we ask or imagine" (Eph 3:20).

PART II

The Sacrament of Holy Orders

The Sacrament of Holy Orders is the sacrament of apostolic ministry, the way that the mission which Christ entrusted to his apostles is carried out in the Church until he returns (CCC, 1536). The three degrees of the Sacrament of Holy Orders—bishop, priest, and deacon—participate in Christ's mission in different but complementary ways. In the next three chapters we will examine how the Sacrament of Holy Orders expresses and effects this sacramental participation in the mission of Christ.

In chapter 4 we will give a brief introduction to the sacrament and then look at the Old Testament roots and types that prefigure the Sacrament of Holy Orders. The rite for each degree of Holy Orders focuses on a different Old Testament figure, Abraham for bishops, Aaron and his sons for priests, and the Levites for deacons. We will also look at some of the key Old Testament readings for the *Rite of Ordination*, especially God's choice of Jeremiah as described in Jeremiah 1:4–9 and Isaiah's prophecy that the Lord will anoint his messenger with the Spirit (61:1–3). Finally, we will reflect on the Old Testament figure of Melchizedek, who prefigures the high priesthood of Christ.

In chapter 5 we will look at the signs that comprise the Sacrament of Holy Orders. Some signs are common to the ordination rite of all three degrees, such as the imposition of hands, the litany of the saints, and postures such as kneeling and prostration. Other signs are specific to each degree, such as handing over the bread and wine to the priest and the ring, miter, and crozier to the bishop. In chapter 6 we will examine how the promises made during the *Rite of Ordination* reveal how the sacrament transforms the life of the ordained minister. At the heart of these promises is the relationship of the ordained to Christ: the deacon promises to conform his life to the example of Christ, the priest promises to be united more closely to Christ, and the bishop promises to build up and remain in unity with the Body of Christ. Rooted in the Old Testament priesthood, celebrated with a diversity of sacramental signs, and becoming in distinct ways a sacramental sign of Christ, bishops and priests (the two degrees of priestly participation) and deacons (the degree of service) continue the saving and sanctifying work of Christ in his Church.

Chapter 4

Holy Orders:
Old Testament Roots

INTRODUCTION: THE PRIESTHOOD OF CHRIST

"We have a great high priest who has passed through the heavens, Jesus, the Son of God" (Heb 4:14). One of the great themes of the Epistle to the Hebrews is the priesthood of Christ. He is a high priest who is "holy, innocent, undefiled" (Heb 7:26), "a merciful and faithful high priest before God" (Heb 2:17) who, through his Paschal Mystery "has made perfect forever those who are being consecrated" (Heb 10:14). "Therefore, holy 'brothers,' sharing in a heavenly calling, reflect on Jesus, the apostle and high priest of our confession" (Heb 3:1).

Obedient to the exhortation in the Epistle to the Hebrews, the Church has reflected on the priesthood of Christ and come to understand that there are two participations in the one priesthood of Christ: the priesthood of all the baptized, and the ministerial priesthood of bishops and priests, assisted by deacons. Through the Sacrament of Baptism Christ has "made us into a kingdom, priests for his God and Father" (Rev 1:6; cf. Rev 5:9–10), so that all the faithful are "a chosen race, a royal priesthood, a holy nation" (1 Pt 2:9). Baptism and Confirmation consecrate the faithful to be "a holy priesthood" (LG, 10). They exercise their priesthood "by a vital participation in the holy liturgy of the Church" and "by the witness of holy lives and practical charity" (CCC, 1273). Complementing the priesthood of the baptized, through the sacrament of Holy Orders, men are configured to Christ as "a *means* by which Christ unceasingly builds up and leads his Church" (CCC, 1547). The ministerial or hierarchical priesthood "is at the service of the common priesthood," to assist the laity in their growth in "a life of faith, hope, and charity, a life according to the Spirit" (CCC, 1547). In this way the faithful and the ordained participate, "each in its own way in the one priesthood of Christ" (LG, 10). While distinct, these two participations in the one priesthood of Christ are intrinsically related.

The name for this sacrament—"Holy Orders"—is taken from ancient Rome, which used the word *ordo* to designate a civil body, in particular a governing body. One was incorporated into an *ordo* through *ordinatio*, from which we get the word ordination. From ancient times the Church has organized bodies into orders: in addition to the order of bishops (*ordo episcoporum*), the order of priests (*ordo presbyterorum*), and the order of deacons (*ordo diaconorum*), she has established orders for groups such as widows, virgins, and catechumens. Members were incorporated into these orders through *ordinatio*, "a religious and liturgical act which was a consecration, a blessing or a sacrament. Today the word '*ordination*' is reserved for the sacramental act which integrates a man into the order of bishops, presbyters, or deacons, and . . . confers a gift of the Holy Spirit that permits the exercise of a 'sacred power' which can come only from Christ himself through his Church. Ordination is also called *consecratio*, for it is a setting apart and an investiture by Christ himself for his Church." (CCC, 1538).

From the earliest days, the Church has recognized three degrees of ordained ministry: bishops (episcopacy), priests (presbyterate), and deacons (diaconate). In the early second century, St. Ignatius of Antioch described these three degrees thus: "Let everyone revere the deacons as Jesus Christ, the bishop as the image of the Father, and the presbyters as the senate of God and the assembly of the apostles. For without them one cannot speak of the Church" (CCC, 1554).

The first two, bishops and priests, are ministerial participations in the priesthood of Christ. As successors of the apostles, bishops receive "the fullness of the sacrament of Orders," so that bishops, "eminently and visibly, take the place of Christ himself, teacher, shepherd and priest, and act in his person" (LG, 21). Each bishop "is 'the steward of the grace of the supreme priesthood,' above all in the Eucharist, which he himself offers, or ensures that it is offered, and by which the church continues to live and grow" (LG, 26). Priests share with bishops the dignity of the priesthood and "depend on the bishops for the exercise of their power" (LG, 28). They are ordained "to preach the Gospel and shepherd the faithful as well as to celebrate divine worship as true priests of the New Testament. . . . Acting in the person of Christ and proclaiming his mystery, they unite the prayers of the faithful to the sacrifice of Christ their head, and in the sacrifice of the Mass they make present again and apply, until the coming of the Lord (see 1 Cor 11:26), the unique sacrifice of the New Testament, Christ offering himself once for all an unblemished victim to the Father (see Heb 9:11–28)" (LG, 28).

While deacons do not receive the ministerial priesthood, through ordination they do receive "important functions in the ministry of the word, divine worship, pastoral governance, and the service of charity, tasks which they must carry out under the pastoral authority of their bishop" (CCC, 1596). It is also worth noting that both the episcopacy (bishops) and the presbyterate (priests) "contain" the diaconate, since both are first ordained to the diaconate; consequently, "they are also ministries of service as well as of mediation."[1] We may summarize the three degrees of Holy Orders as follows: "the deacon mediates the Word of God, the priest the Word and the Eucharist; the bishop mediates the Word, the Eucharist and the Church."[2] All three degrees are conferred by the sacrament of Holy Orders.

THE STRUCTURE OF THE SACRAMENT

Since the Sacrament of Holy Orders "is the sacrament of the apostolic ministry, it is for the bishops as the successors of the apostles to hand on the 'gift of the Spirit'" (CCC, 1576). Only a baptized man can be ordained. The sacrament is always conferred by the bishop within celebration of Mass "in which the faithful, particularly on a Sunday, take an active part 'at one altar at which the Bishop presides, surrounded by his presbyterate and ministers'" (RO, 9).[3] In this way the preeminent manifestation of the Church and the conferral of Holy Orders are joined to the Eucharistic Sacrifice, the font and apex of the whole Christian life" (RO, 9). The celebration of the Eucharist by the bishop with his priests and deacons is the preeminent manifestation of the Church because "in the most blessed Eucharist is contained the entire spiritual wealth of the church, namely Christ himself," and the bishop

---

1. Paul Haffner, *The Sacramental Mystery*, rev. ed. (Herefordshire: Gracewing, 2007), 211.

2. Ibid., 211.

3. St. John Paul II, in an address to priests, noted the intrinsic relationship between ordination and the Eucharist: "*Through our ordination*—the celebration of which is linked to the holy Mass from the very first liturgical evidence—we are united in a singular and exceptional way to the Eucharist" (*Dominicae Cenae*, 2; italics original).

"eminently and visibly, take[s] the place of Christ himself, teacher, shepherd and priest, and act[s] in his person" (PO, 5; LG, 21).

The *Rite of Ordination* begins during the Liturgy of the Word, following the reading of the Gospel. It is comprised of three parts. The first part consists of the preparatory rites: the presentation of the one(s) to be ordained, the Homily, the Promise of the Elect, and the Litany of Supplication. This is followed by the essential element of ordination— the laying on of hands and the Prayer of Ordination, which "specifies the signification of the laying on of hands" (RO, 7). It concludes with the explanatory rites, "which are different for the various Orders and which represent the offices that have been conferred through the laying on of hands and the invocation of the Holy Spirit" (RO, 8). In the explanatory rites, signs and symbols are given that "explain" the office just conferred. For the ordination of the bishop, this includes the giving of the ring, the miter and the crozier (pastoral staff); for the priesthood, the handing over of bread and wine; and for the diaconate, the handing on of the Book of the Gospels. The structure of the *Rite of Ordination* is summarized in the chart below.

Figure 4.1 The Sacrament of Holy Orders

Bishop	Priest	Deacon
Gospel	Gospel	Gospel
Presentation of the Elect	Election of Candidates	Election of Candidates
Homily	Homily	Homily
Promise of Elect	Promise of Elect	Promise of Elect
Litany of Saints	Litany of Saints	Litany of Saints
Laying on of Hands	Laying on of Hands	Laying on of Hands
Prayer of Ordination	Prayer of Ordination	Prayer of Ordination
	Vesting stole and chasuble	**Vesting stole and dalmatic**
Anointing of Head	**Anointing Hands**	**Handing on Book of Gospels**
Handing on Gospels	**Handing over Bread/ Wine**	
Insignia (ring, miter, crozier)		
Occupies *Cathedra*		
Fraternal Kiss		
Liturgy of Eucharist with inserts	Liturgy of Eucharist with inserts	Liturgy of Eucharist with inserts

OLD TESTAMENT ROOTS OF THE SACRAMENT OF HOLY ORDERS

As we explained in the previous chapter, the first aspect of a mysta-gogical catechesis is a consideration of the Old Testament roots of the sacrament. The first and most important starting point is the liturgy itself, as the *Catechism* notes: "The liturgy of the Church . . . sees in the priesthood of Aaron and the service of the Levites, as in the institution of the seventy elders (cf. Nm 11:24–25), a prefiguring of the ordained ministry of the New Covenant" (CCC, 1541). As we will see below, the *Rite of Ordination* for each of the degrees, (episcopacy, presbyterate, and diaconate), makes reference to these Old Testament figures and events.

The Old Testament readings chosen for each of the degrees of Holy Orders are a second important source of information about the Old Testament roots of the sacrament. Here it is worth recalling what we said in chapter 1 about the Word of God: the Word of God manifests the presence of Christ. "Always, however, Christ is present in his word, as he carries out the mystery of salvation, he sanctifies humanity and offers the Father perfect worship" (GIL, 4). This is true not only of the New Testament, but equally so of the Old Testament. "When in cele-brating the Liturgy the Church proclaims both the Old and New Testament, it is proclaiming the one and the same mystery of Christ. . . . Christ himself is the center and fullness of the whole of Scripture, just as he is of all liturgical celebration" (GIL, 5). Furthermore, when the Word is proclaimed in the liturgy, "he expects a response, one that is, of listening and adoring 'in Spirit and in truth' (Jn 4:23). The Holy Spirit makes the response effective, so that what is heard in the celebration of the Liturgy may be carried out in a way of life: 'Be doers of the word and not hearers only' (Jas 1:22)" (GIL 6). Here we also see again the Trinitarian nature of the liturgy: the Father calls us to respond to the Word of his Son, made effective in our lives through the working of the Holy Spirit. "The word of God constantly proclaimed in the Liturgy is always, then a living and effective word through the power of the Holy Spirit. It expresses the Father's love that never fails in its effectiveness toward us" (GIL, 4).

While there are specific Old Testament readings for each of three degrees of Holy Orders, there is one that is common to all three: Jeremiah 1:4–9. This passage describes Jeremiah's call—"before you were born"—to be "a prophet to the nations" (v. 5). The choice is God's, not Jeremiah's. This is equally true of the sacrament: "No one has a *right* to receive the sacrament of Holy Orders. Indeed no one claims this office for himself; he is called to it by God" (CCC, 1578, citing Heb 5:4). When Jeremiah protests that he is too young, God assures him that he will give him the words to speak: "See, I place my words in your mouth" (v. 9). He also assures the young prophet of his presence and support: "I am with you to deliver you" (v. 8). This Old Testament passage is appropriate for ordination to all three degrees because it emphasizes God's choice of his ordained ministers and because each mediates the word of God to the people of God in ways appropriate to each office.

In the sections that follow we will explore the Old Testament roots of the episcopacy, presbyterate, and diaconate by looking at the Old Testament references in the Prayer of Ordination for each of the degrees (bishop, priest, and deacon) and the Old Testament readings proposed for each degree.

BISHOP

The Prayer of Ordination for bishops cites God's promise to Abraham, the institution of rulers and priests, and his provision for ministers of the sanctuary.

> Father of mercies and God of all consolation . . .
> who from the beginning,
> foreordained a nation of the just,
> born of Abraham:
> who established rulers and priests
> and did not leave your sanctuary without ministers . . . (RO, 47)

The reference to "a nation of the just born of Abraham" is found in Genesis 12, God's choice of Abraham. God tells Abraham to leave his country and go to a place that God will show him. And he promises to bless Abraham and to make of him "a great nation" so that in him "all the families of the earth will find blessing" (12:2–3). Prefigured in this promise is the definitive blessing of salvation in Christ, visibly manifested in the person of the bishop. The prayer also makes reference to the establishment of "rulers and priests" as well as ministers for the sanctuary, events described in the books of Exodus, Leviticus, and Numbers. The Prayer of Ordination for priests and deacons respectively contain more specific references to these events, so we will discuss the relevant passages in those sections.

One of the Old Testament readings for the ordination of both bishops and priests is Isaiah 61:1–3abcd. In this passage the prophet announces that the spirit of the Lord is upon him, and in a messianic ("messiah" means "the anointed one") reference proclaims that the Lord has anointed him. He is the messenger of the Lord "to bring good news to the afflicted, to bind up the brokenhearted, to proclaim liberty to the captives, release to the prisoners, To announce a year of favor from the LORD and a day of vindication by our God; To comfort all who mourn; to place on those who mourn in Zion a diadem instead of ashes, To give them oil of gladness instead of mourning, a glorious mantle instead of a faint spirit" (61:2–3).

An analysis of this passage reveals several ways in which it prefigures the priesthood of the new covenant.[4] The reference to the spirit "signals the special action of God (Jgs 3:10; 11:19; 1 Sm 10:5–13)." While other Old Testament prophecies spoke of the spirit with reference to the messianic king (Is 11:1–2) and promised it to the messianic people (Jl 3; Zec 12:10), here the spirit is given to anoint prophecy. The term *anointed* "is linked with preaching and hearing; it designates an interior enlightening to know God's word and a strengthening to follow it." The phrase "release to prisoners" can also be translated as "light to prisoners." In either case, "prisoners are led out of dark dungeons to full daylight." This passage "looks to the total salvation of God's people—bodily and spiritually, individually and socially." Finally, the reference to "the day of vindication of the Lord" is almost always used to describe God "repairing the injured or weakened force of salvation (34:8; 59:17)."[5]

This Old Testament prophecy is definitively fulfilled in the ministry of Jesus. In the Gospel of Luke, Jesus inaugurates his public ministry by reading this passage in the synagogue on the Sabbath. After proclaiming this passage, Jesus announces that he is the one about whom Isaiah prophesied: "Today this scripture passage is fulfilled in your hearing" (Lk 4:21). "With these words Jesus announced that the

---

4. This analysis is taken from Raymond E. Brown, Joseph Fitzmyer, and Roland Murphy, eds., *New Jerome Biblical Commentary*, (Upper Saddle River, NJ: Prentice Hall, 1990), 346.

5. Raymond Brown et al., eds., *New Jerome Biblical Commentary*, 346.

messianic era had come."[6] In his words and deeds Christ brought good news to the poor and oppressed, comforted the brokenhearted, brought freedom to those oppressed by the enemy, and freed those imprisoned by illness—the blind saw the salvation of the Lord, the deaf heard the good news, and the mute praised the Lord. God's saving action, hindered by the corruption and self-interest of the religious establishment of Jesus' day, was fully and definitively realized in Christ.

This passage has a particular relevance for the ordination of both bishops and priests, who by virtue of ordination are configured to Christ so that "it is Christ himself who is present to his Church as Head of his Body, Shepherd of his flock, high priest of the redemptive sacrifice, Teacher of Truth" (CCC, 1548). This is what the Church means when she says that the priest (and the bishop was first a priest) acts "in the person of Christ the head" (the Latin phrase is *in persona Christi Capitis*). Through priestly ordination the minister "is truly made like to the high priest and possesses the authority to act in the power and place of the person of Christ himself" (Pius XII quoted in CCC, 1548). In St. Thomas Aquinas' elegant summary, "Christ is the source of all priesthood: the priest of the old law was a figure of Christ, and the priest of the new law acts in the person of Christ" (quoted in CCC, 1548).

Old Testament: Episcopal Ordination

Compare Isaiah 61:1–3 to the servant songs of Isaiah: 42:1–4; 49:1–7; 50:4–11; and 52:13—53:12. What similarities do you see? Look for references to anointing by the Spirit, a mission of mercy, and a year of favor.

PRIEST

The Prayer of Ordination for priests contains several Old Testament references. It first mentions ministerial offices in the old covenant that were "established through mystical rites." It then mentions those appointed to assist Moses and Aaron.

> Already in the earlier covenant
> offices arose, established through mystical rites:
> when you set Moses and Aaron over your people

---

6. Raymond Brown et al., eds., *New Jerome Biblical Commentary*, 346.

> to govern and sanctify them,
> you chose men next in rank and dignity
> to accompany them and assist them in their task. (RO, 130)

The "mystical rites" for the consecration of the Old Testament priests are described in Exodus 29:1–30, the consecration of Aaron and his sons. Aaron is vested in a tunic, ephod, breast piece and embroidered belt, and a turban with the sacred diadem is placed on his head. Anointing oil is then poured on his head. His sons are clothed with tunics and sashes and skullcaps on their heads. "Thus shall the priesthood be theirs by a perpetual statute, and thus shall you install Aaron and his sons" (v. 9). This is followed by the sacrifice of "a young bull and two unblemished rams" (v. 1). The blood of the sacrifices is splashed on and around the altar and used to anoint the tip of the right ears of Aaron and his sons, as well as "the thumbs of their right hands and the great toes of their right feet" (v. 20). The meat, hide, and dung of the bull are burned outside the camp as a purification offering (v. 14), and one of the rams is burned on the altar as "a sweet-smelling oblation" (v. 18). The blood of the other ram that is splashed on the altar and together with anointing oil is sprinkled on Aaron and his sons and on their vestments "that he and his sons and their vestments may be sacred" (v. 21). Parts of the ram along with a loaf of unleavened bread, a cake made with oil and a wafer are then given to Aaron and his sons who "raise them as an elevated offering before the LORD" (v. 24). They are then burned on the altar "as a sweet-smelling oblation to the LORD" (v. 25).

The consecration of Aaron's sons is mentioned in another section of the Prayer of Ordination:

> So also upon the sons of Aaron
> you poured an abundant share of their father's plenty,
> that the number of the priests prescribed by the Law
> might be sufficient for the sacrifices of the tabernacle,
> which were a shadow of the good things to come. (RO, 130)

This reference concludes with an explanation of the importance of the Old Testament for understanding the offices of the new covenant—they "were a shadow of the good things to come." This "mystical" rite prefigures many elements of the current *Rite of Ordination*: the divine choice of the ministers, clothing with sacred vestments, anointing with oil, and the offering of sacrifices.

The Prayer of Ordination also refers to those chosen to assist Moses and Aaron. This is found in Exodus 18:17–27. Moses' father-in-law tells him that his responsibilities are too great for him to bear alone. He advises him to choose "able and God-fearing men, trustworthy men who hate dishonest gain" who can then "render decisions for the people in all routine cases" (Ex 18:21–22). He urges Moses to do this—on the condition that "God so commands you"—so that he "will be able to stand the strain, and all these people, too, will go home content" (Ex 18:23). This prefigures the pastoral ministry of priests as assistants to the bishops.

The Prayer of Ordination next mentions the seventy elders who received the spirit to assist Moses:

> So too in the desert
> you implanted the spirit of Moses
> in the hearts of seventy wise men;
> and with their help he ruled your people with greater ease.
> (RO, 159)

This event is described in Numbers 11:10–29. When the people complain about the food in the desert, Moses complains to the Lord: "Why are you so displeased with me that you burden me with all this people? . . . I cannot carry all this people by myself, for they are too heavy for me" (vv. 11, 14). God replies by telling Moses to gather "seventy of the elders of Israel, whom you know to be elders and authorities among the people" (16). Then, when they are all assembled at the tent of meeting, God tells Moses, "I will also take some of the spirit that is on you and will confer it on them, that they may share the burden of the people with you. You will then not have to bear it by yourself" (17). When the spirit was bestowed on the seventy, "they prophesied but did not continue" (25). This prefigures the gift of the spirit bestowed on the priests as coworkers with the bishop. This passage is one of the Old Testament readings for the ordination of priests, which reflects its importance as prefiguring the priesthood of the new covenant.

The Old Testament references in the *Rite of Ordination* of Priests reveal key elements of the rite, especially the relationship between ordination and sacrifice. They also anticipate the pastoral ministry of priests and the gift of the Spirit. Finally, they reveal the collegiality of the priesthood.

DEACON

The Prayer of Ordination for deacons cites the Lord's choice of the sons of Levi as prefiguring the three degrees of ministers in the new covenant:

> as once you chose the sons of Levi
> to minister in the former tabernacle,
> so now you establish three ranks of ministers
> in their sacred offices to serve in your name. (RO, 207)

God's choice of the sons of Levi is recorded in Numbers 1:48–53. God tells Moses not to include the Levites "in the census along with the other Israelites" (49). Rather, they are to have "charge of the tabernacle of the covenant with all its equipment and all that belongs to it" and "shall be its ministers" (50). Because God designated the tribe of Levi for liturgical service, "God himself is its inheritance" (CCC, 1539). The Levites' ministry is further described in one of the Old Testament readings for the ordination of deacons as recorded in Numbers 3:5–9. In this passage the Lord tells Moses to station the Levites "before Aaron the priest to serve him" (6). They are responsible for all of the furnishings of the tent of meeting and for maintaining the tabernacle. They are "assigned unconditionally" to Aaron and his sons (9).

This passage prefigures an important aspect of the diaconate, the liturgical ministry of deacons. Just as the Levites were assigned to assist Aaron and his sons, so men are ordained to the diaconate "so as to serve as a vested minister in the sanctification of the Christian community, in hierarchical communion with the bishop and priests. They provide a sacramental assistance to the ministry of the bishop and, subordinately, to that of the priests which is intrinsic, fundamental and distinct" (DMLPD, 28). Their ministry at the altar is distinct both from the liturgical ministry of the lay faithful and from that of the ministerial priesthood (DMLPD, 28). So, for example, "in the Eucharistic Sacrifice, the deacon does not celebrate the mystery: rather, he effectively represents on the one hand, the people of God and, specifically, helps them to unite their lives to the offering of Christ; while on the other, in the name of Christ himself, he helps the Church to participate in the fruits of that sacrifice" (DMLPD, 28).

MELCHIZEDEK

While the priesthood of the Old Testament prefigures in many ways the priesthood of Christ—proclaiming the Word of God and restoring "communion with God by sacrifices and prayer (cf. Mal 2:7–9), this priesthood nevertheless remains powerless to bring about salvation, needing to repeat its sacrifices ceaselessly and being unable to achieve a definitive sanctification, which only the sacrifice of Christ would accomplish" (CCC, 1540). The Old Testament figure who most clearly points to the priesthood of Christ is Melchizedek.

Melchizedek is first mentioned in Genesis 14:17–24 when he meets Abraham who has just defeated Chedorlaomer and his allies. He is mentioned again in Psalm 110: "The LORD has sworn and will not waver: 'You are a priest forever in the manner of Melchizedek'" (4). From these Old Testament passages the Epistle to the Hebrews explains how Melchizedek prefigures the priesthood of Christ. "The Christian tradition considers Melchizedek, 'priest of God Most High,' as a prefiguration of the priesthood of Christ, the unique 'high priest after the order of Melchizedek' (Heb 5:10; cf. 6:20; Gn 14:18); 'holy, blameless, unstained' (Heb 7:26), 'by a single offering he has perfected for all time those who are sanctified' (Heb 10:14), that is, by the unique sacrifice of the cross" (CCC, 1544).

The New Testament reflection on Melchizedek is an example of what the Church calls "rereadings," reflections by the New Testament writers on Old Testament events and figures that reflect the unity of the two testaments. "One thing that gives the Bible an inner unity, unique of its kind, is the fact that later biblical writings often depend upon earlier ones. These more recent writings allude to older ones, create 'rereadings' (relectures) which develop new aspects of meaning, sometimes quite different from the original sense. A text may also make explicit reference to older passages, whether it is to deepen their meaning or to make known their fulfillment."[7]

In the case of Melchizedek, the writer of Hebrews reflects on both Old Testament sources, summarizing the account in Genesis 14 and quoting Psalm 110:6 three times (5:6; 7:17, 21): "You are a priest forever according to the order of Melchizedek." As this suggests, one of his

---

7. The Pontifical Biblical Commission, *The Interpretation of the Bible in the Church*, (Boston: Pauline Books and Media, 1994), 90.

emphases is the eternal priesthood of Melchizedek prefiguring the eternal priesthood of Christ. The other theme he stresses is a change of priesthood, from the order of Aaron to that of Melchizedek. "If, then, perfection came through the levitical priesthood, on the basis of which the people received the law, what need would there still have been for another priest to arise according to the order of Melchizedek, and not reckoned according to the order of Aaron? . . . It is even more obvious if another priest is raised up after the likeness of Melchizedek, who has become so, not by a law expressed in a commandment concerning physical descent but by the power of a life that cannot be destroyed" (7:11–12, 15–16).

Finding Melchizedek

Melchizedek is described in Genesis 14:17–24, Psalm 110, and Hebrews 5–7. Read these passages. How does each develop the idea of Melchizedek's priesthood? Also, review the discussion in chapter 3 (pp. 44–45) of the reference to Melchizedek in Eucharistic Prayer I.

The Church Fathers' interpretations of Christ as a priest forever according to the order of Melchizedek reveal the multifaceted aspects of this truth. For St. Augustine, it prefigured the Eucharist now offered on altars throughout the world: "Here we certainly see the first manifestation of the sacrifice which is now offered to God by Christians in the whole world, in which is fulfilled what was said in prophecy, long after this event, to Christ who was yet to come in the Flesh: 'you are a priest forever, after the order of Melchizedek.'"[8] The sacrifice "now offered in the whole world" is a reference to Malachi 1:11 and is found in the liturgy itself: "you never cease to gather a people to yourself, so that from the rising of the sun to its setting, a pure sacrifice may be offered to your name" (RM, Eucharistic Prayer III).

Braulio of Saragossa saw in Melchizedek's offering of bread and wine a prefigurement of the Eucharistic sacrifice, for "through the sacrament, bread and wine offered to God become for us the true body and blood of Christ, according to the words of the Lord himself and the sacred Scriptures composed by the Holy Spirit. This sacrament the

---

8. Erik M. Heen and Philip D. W. Krey, *Hebrews*, Ancient Christian Commentary on Scripture (Downers Grove, IL: InterVarsity Press, 2005), 96.

Catholic church offers daily on its altar 'after the order of Melchizedek' by the true pontiff, Jesus Christ, with mystical understanding and an ineffable dearth of speech, because surpassing grace goes beyond everything."[9] Like St. Augustine, he also noted the worldwide offering of the Eucharist.

St. Epiphanius of Salamis offers a comprehensive summary of Christ's eternal priesthood in the order of Melchizedek, beginning with the Incarnation: "He had taken his substance from man so as to be made a priest for us after the order of Melchizedek, which has no succession." As a result, Christ "abides forever to offer gifts for us—after first offering himself by the cross, to abolish every sacrifice of the old covenant by presenting the more perfect, living sacrifice for the whole world. He himself is temple, sacrifice, priest, altar, God, man, king, high priest, lamb, sacrificial victim—become all in all for us that life may be ours in every way and to lay the changeless foundation of his priesthood forever, no longer allotting it by descent and succession but granting that, in accordance with his ordinance, it may be preserved in the Holy Spirit."[10] This is luminous passage, touching on the Incarnation, temple, priesthood, and sacrifice, and in the reference to a "priesthood . . . preserved in the Holy Spirit,"[11] the Sacrament of Holy Orders, it reveals the unity of the Bible and the richness of Christ's eternal priesthood.

CONCLUSION

The Old Testament provides a rich theological and ritual foundation for the Sacrament of Holy Orders. The consecration of Aaron and his sons through "mystical rites" prefigures the structure and key elements of the ordination of priests, while the service of the Levites foreshadows the diaconal ministry. The Old Testament readings articulate a rich theology of ordained ministry. And the priesthood of Melchizedek provides the type for the high priesthood of Christ.

---

9. Ibid., 115.
10. Ibid., 99.
11. Ibid.

Chapter 5

Holy Orders: Signs and Symbols

INTRODUCTION

As we have seen, sacramental celebrations are composed of liturgical signs that engage the whole person and communicate the power of Christ's Paschal Mystery. The liturgical signs that comprise the Sacrament of Holy Orders are complex and varied. They include the postures of standing, kneeling, and prostration and gestures such as the imposition of hands and the fraternal kiss. The Church Triumphant is invoked through the Litany of Supplication. Bishops and priests are anointed with sacred Chrism, a sign of the Holy Spirit. The newly ordained are clothed with rich vestments that signify their sacred ministry. Signs such as the miter, chalice and paten, and the Book of the Gospels are given to signify the distinctive participation of each degree in the one priesthood of Christ. In this chapter we will look closely at the signs of the Sacrament of Holy Orders so that we can "pass from its signs to the mystery they contain" and so enter more deeply into this sacramental mystery.

As we discussed in the last chapter, the Rite of Ordination consists of three parts that express "the multiple aspects of sacramental grace" (CCC, 1574). The first part consists of the preparatory rites: the presentation of the one(s) to be ordained, the Homily, the Promise of the Elect, and the Litany of Supplication. These rites "attest that the choice of the candidate is made in keeping with the practice of the Church and prepare for the solemn act of consecration" (CCC, 1574). This is followed by the essential Rite of Ordination: the laying on of hands and the Prayer of Ordination (also referred to as the consecratory prayer). As we noted in chapter 2, if the essential rite is omitted or altered, the sacrament is invalid. The Rite of Ordination concludes with the explanatory rites that "symbolically express and complete the mystery accomplished" (CCC, 1574). In considering the signs that comprise the Rite of Ordination, we will look first at the rite itself, supplemented by the *General Instruction of the Rite of Ordination* and the *Catechism*. Below is a chart of the Rite of Ordination for all three degrees. The preparatory rites are given in a regular font, the essential element in italics, and the explanatory rites in bold. Also included is the gesture or posture that accompanies the different elements.

Figure 5.1 The Sacrament of Holy Orders

Bishop	Priest	Deacon
Gospel	Gospel	Gospel
Presentation of the Elect (led to Bishop, makes sign of reverence)	Election of Candidates (goes to bishop, sign of reverence)	Election of Candidates
Homily	Homily	Homily
Promise of Elect (stands before bishop)	Promise of Elect (stand before the bishop)	Promise of Elect
Litany of Saints (prostrates)	Litany of Saints (elect prostrate)	Litany of Saints
Laying on of Hands (kneels before bishop)	*Laying on of Hands* (kneel before bishop)	*Laying on of Hands*
Prayer of Ordination (deacons hold book of Gospels over head)	*Prayer of Ordination*	*Prayer of Ordination*
	(stands) **Vesting with Stole and Chasuble**	**Vesting with Stole and Dalmatic**
Anointing of Head (kneels)	**Anointing Hands (kneels before bishop)**	**Handing on Book of Gospels (kneels)**
Handing on Gospels	**Handing over Bread and Wine (kneels before bishop)**	
Insignia (ring, miter, crozier) (rises)	**Fraternal kiss**	
Occupies *Cathedra*		
Fraternal kiss		
Liturgy of Eucharist with inserts	Liturgy of Eucharist with inserts	Liturgy of Eucharist with inserts

> ## Festive Colors
>
> The Rite of Ordination is ordinarily celebrated with "the color white or a festive color" (*Roman Missal*). Review the discussion of liturgical colors in chapter 2. Why is the color white preferred for ordinations? What are approved festive colors?

PREPARATORY RITE: THE ELECTION OF CANDIDATES

The Rite of Ordination for Priests and Deacons begins with the election of candidates. Following the reading of the Gospel but before the homily, a deacon calls the candidate by name: "Let N., who is to be ordained a Priest, come forward." The candidate responds, "Present," and makes a sign of reverence to the bishop. The rite does not specify the exact nature of this sign of reverence, but in the United States it is customary for the candidate to stand when his name is called, answer "Present," and make a slight bow to the bishop.

The posture of standing has several meanings within the context of the liturgy: "One rises to greet people, to honor someone important, or to express readiness for action, or when seized with excitement. In Christian liturgical tradition, standing is the basic posture of an Easter people lifted up to greet their risen Lord" (IOM, 29). Cardinal Ratzinger explains standing as the posture proper to an Easter people: "Standing is the posture of the victor. Jesus stands in God's presence—he stands, because he has trodden death and the power of the Evil One underfoot. At the end of this struggle, he is the one who stands upright, the one who remains standing. This standing is also an expression of readiness: Christ is standing up at the right hand of God, in order to meet us. . . . When we stand, we know that we are united to the victory of Christ. . . . "[1]. The candidate expresses his readiness to be ordained not only by responding "Present," but also by his posture, standing before the bishop.

The rite continues with a designated priest saying to the bishop, "Most Reverend Father, holy mother Church asks you to ordain N., our brother, to the responsibility of the Priesthood." The bishop inquires about the candidate's worthiness, and the priest replies, "After inquiry

---

1. Joseph Ratzinger, *The Spirit of the Liturgy* (San Francisco: Ignatius, 200), 195.

among the Christian people and upon the recommendation of those responsible, I testify that he has been found worthy." The bishop then confirms his election: "Relying on the help of the Lord God and our Savior Jesus Christ, we choose N., our brother, for the Order of the Priesthood." The assembly then gives their assent. In the Dioceses of the United States, this assent can take different forms: a sung or recited acclamation such as "Thanks be to God" or by an action such as applause or standing. The liturgy then continues with the homily.

PREPARATORY RITE: LITANY OF SUPPLICATION

Common to the preparatory rites for all three degrees of Holy Orders is the Litany of Supplication, also known as the Litany of the Saints. A litany is a form of prayer consisting of a series of petitions, said or sung, with a fixed response, such as "Lord, have mercy" or "pray for us." It is divided into two parts: a series of petitions addressed directly to God, and the invocation of a series of saints. The origins of this prayer are obscure, although there are examples from Jewish and pagan sources. The litany was used in the early Church before the dismissal of the catechumens (those preparing for Baptism), who did not participate in the prayers of the faithful. There is evidence that this litanic prayer form was used in Rome before 225. In addition to the Rite of Ordination, litanies are part of other liturgical celebrations such as the Sacraments of Baptism and the Easter Vigil. They are also part of private devotions, such as the Litany of the Sacred Heart and the Litany of Loreto.

The Litany of Supplication is an example of the union of the earthly Church with the heavenly Church that occurs in every liturgical celebration. The liturgy, as we noted in chapter 2, is unceasingly celebrated in heaven by Christ, our high priest, "with the holy Mother of God, the apostles, all the saints, and the multitude of those who have already entered the kingdom" (CCC, 1187). When we celebrate the liturgy, we are "entering into the liturgy of the heavens that has always been taking place. Earthly liturgy is liturgy because and only because it joins what is already in process, the greater reality."[2] We seek the intercession of the saints because they are present at our liturgical celebrations, and their intercession is efficacious.

---

2. Joseph Ratzinger, *A New Song to the Lord: Faith in Christ and Liturgy Today*, trans. Martha M. Matesich (New York: Crossroad, 1996), 166.

The Litany of the Saints has been part of the Rite of Ordination from the seventh century onward "in preparation for the imposition of hands, so as to invoke the assistance of the saints on behalf of those about to be ordained."[3] Beginning in the eighth century, the candidates prostrated themselves during the litany.[4] St. John Paul II described his experience of this rite as an ordinand and as the presider as bishop and pope: "There is something very impressive about the prostration of the ordinands, symbolizing as it does their total submission before the majesty of God and their complete openness to the action of the Holy Spirit who will descend upon them and consecrate them."[5] Prostration gives bodily expression to "the awareness of our absolute incapacity, by our own powers, to take on the priestly mission of Jesus Christ, to speak with his 'I.'"[6]

Cardinal Ratzinger described his experience of the Litany of the Saints during his episcopal ordination: "The fact that the praying Church was calling upon the saints, that the prayer of the Church really was enveloping and embracing me, was a wonderful consolation. In my incapacity, which had to be expressed in the bodily posture of prostration, this prayer, this presence of all the saints, of the living and the dead, was a wonderful strength—it was the only thing that could, as it were, lift me up. Only the presence of the saints with me made possible the path that lay before me."[7] The Litany of the Saints in the Rite of Ordination illustrates how the liturgy integrates different signs—words, music, and posture—to signify sacramental realities and engage the whole person.

THE ESSENTIAL RITE: LAYING ON OF HANDS AND PRAYER OF ORDINATION

The essential rite and visible sign "for all three degrees consists in the bishop's imposition of hands on the head of the ordinand and in the bishop's specific consecratory prayer asking God for the outpouring of the Holy Spirit and his gifts proper to the ministry to which the candidate is being ordained" (CCC, 1573). The imposition of hands is rooted

---

3. James Monti, *A Sense of the Sacred: Roman Catholic Worship in the Middle Ages* (San Francisco: Ignatius, 2012), 163.

4. Ibid. During the Easter Season, the congregation remains standing; at other times, they kneel during the Litany.

5. John Paul II, *Gift and Mystery: On the Fiftieth Anniversary of My Priestly Ordination* (New York: Doubleday, 1996), 43–44.

6. Ratzinger, *The Spirit of the Liturgy*, 188.

7. Ibid.

in the practice of Jesus himself. He healed the sick and blessed children by laying hands on them (Mk 6:5; 8:23, 10:16), and he empowered the apostles to do the same (Mk 16:18; Acts 5:12; 14:3). In the Acts of the Apostles, the Holy Spirit is imparted through the imposition of hands (Acts 8:17–19; 13:3; 19:6; cf. 1 Tm and 2 Tm). "The imposition of hands," wrote St. John Paul II, "is the continuation of the gesture used by the early Church to signify that the Holy Spirit is being given for a specific mission (cf. Acts 6:6, 8:17, 13:3). Paul imposed hands on the disciple Timothy (cf. 2 Tm 1:6; 1 Tim 4:14), and the gesture has remained in the Church (cf. 1 Tm 5:22) as the efficacious sign of the Holy Spirit's active presence in the Sacrament of Holy Orders.[8]" The Letter to the Hebrews describes the laying on of hands as one of the "'fundamental elements' of its teaching. The Church has kept this sign of the all-powerful out-pouring of the Holy Spirit in its sacramental epicleses" (CCC, 699). St. John Chrysostom explains the sacramental reality of this liturgical sign: "the hand of the man is laid upon (the person) but the whole work is of God, and it is his hand that touches the head of the one ordained, if he be duly ordained."[9]

For example, for the ordination of a bishop, after the principal ordaining bishop has laid his hands on the head of the elect in silence, each of the other bishops present does the same. For the ordination of priests, after the bishop has imposed hands, all of the priests who are present, wearing stoles, lay hands on the elect in silence. "While the laying on of hands is taking place the faithful should pray silently. They take part in the Prayer of Ordination by listening to it and by affirming and concluding it through their final acclamation" (RO, 7). This is a good example of how Christ, Head (bishops and priests) and Body (the faithful), acts in the sacraments.

Epiclesis

Review the section on the epiclesis in chapter 1.

The silent imposition of hands is followed by "the bishop's specific consecratory prayer asking God for the outpouring of the Holy

---

8. John Paul II, *Gift and Mystery*, 44.

9. Quoted in Dumitru Stanliloae, *The Sanctifying Mysteries*, The Experience of God: Orthodox Dogmatic Theology, vol. 5, trans. and ed. Ioan Ionita and Robert Barringer (Brookline, MA: Holy Cross Orthodox Press, 2012), 164.

Spirit and his gifts proper to the ministry to which the candidate is being ordained" (CCC, 1573). Each consecratory prayer implores the gift of the Spirit in a manner specific to the ministry—diaconate, priesthood, or episcopacy—being conferred. Thus, the essential words[10] of the Prayer of Ordination for bishops are, "Pour out now upon these chosen ones that power which is from you, the governing Spirit, whom you gave to your beloved Son, Jesus Christ, the Spirit whom he bestowed upon the holy Apostles, who established the Church in each place as your sanctuary for the glory and unceasing praise of your name." The Spirit is given to bishops to carry on the governing work of the holy Apostles.

The Prayer of Ordination for bishops is accompanied by an additional sign. Following the imposition of hands, the principal ordaining bishop (there are three) places the Book of the Gospels, open, on the head of bishop-elect. Two deacons standing on either side of the bishop-elect then hold the Book of the Gospels above his until the end of the Prayer of Ordination. This gesture is first attested in Syria about the year 380. It is described in a text from the late fifth century: "When a bishop is ordained, two bishops should place and hold the book of the Gospels upon his neck."[11] It seems to stem from the interpretation by the Church Fathers of Exodus 28:9–12, which prescribes that the names of the twelve tribes of Israel be engraved on two onyx stones—six on each stone—that are affixed to the shoulders of Aaron's ephod so that he may "bear their names before the Lord upon both shoulders, for a remembrance" (Ex 28:12). The third century priest and martyr St. Hippolytus of Rome applied this passage to Christ, "the Priest of God most high and invisible, who in the last times has taken upon himself the revelations and the truth, with the long robe [i.e., the ephod], bearing on his two shoulders the two Testaments—the 'Revelations' (the Law) [and] the 'Truth' (the Gospel)—so that he should appear the perfect Priest of the perfect Father." [12] Since the bishop is the visible manifestation of Christ the high priest, this sacramental act signifies

---

10. As was mentioned in chapter 2, the essential words are those words which "belong to the nature of the rite and are consequently required for the validity of the act" (Introduction, *Ordination of Deacons*, n. 187), in other words, these words are necessary for the conferral of the sacrament. If these words are not said, then the sacrament has not been conferred and the candidate has not been ordained.

11. Statuta, quoted in Monti, *A Sense of the Sacred,* 187.

12. Ibid.

Hippolytus' comparison and manifests the bishop's responsibility and authority to faithfully teach the fullness of God's revelation.

The essential words for the ordination of priests are, "Grant, we pray, Almighty Father, to these your servants the dignity of the Priesthood; renew deep within them the Spirit of holiness; may they henceforth possess this office, which comes from you, O God, and is next in rank to the office of Bishop; and by the example of their manner of life, may they instill right conduct" (RO, 131). The Spirit is given to priests to enable them to participate in the specifically priestly ministry of Christ, to progress in holiness, and to inspire holiness in others through their manner of life. Finally, the essential words for the ordination of deacons are, "Send forth upon them, Lord, we pray, the Holy Spirit, that they may be strengthened by the gift of your sevenfold grace for the faithful carrying out of the work of the ministry." Deacons are strengthened by the sevenfold gifts of the Spirit for ministry and service. The essential words of the Prayer of Ordination specify those gifts of the Spirit imparted to each degree.

For the imposition of hands and the Prayer of Ordination, those being ordained kneel before the bishop. Kneeling as a liturgical sign has many meanings. In Old Testament thought, the knees were a symbol of strength: "to bend the knee is, therefore, to bend our strength before the living God, an acknowledgement of the fact that all that we are we receive from him."[13] In several Old Testament passages—2 Chr 6:13; Ezr 9:5; Ps 22:30—it is also an expression of worship. In the Middle Ages it was also a sign of homage.[14] "One kneels as a human gesture of submission. In Christian tradition, kneeling is an acknowledgment of one's creatureliness before God. It can signify penitence for sin, humility, reverence, and adoration" (IOM, 31). As the prescribed posture for the Litany of the Saints, it combines several of these meanings: it acknowledges that the gifts and strength imparted through ordination are God's; it signifies the obedience of priests and deacons to the bishop; and it is a sign of humility before the greatness of the ministry being conferred.

---

13. Ratzinger, *The Spirit of the Liturgy*, 191.

14. United States Conference of Catholic Bishops, *Praying with Body, Mind, and Voice* (Washington, DC: United States Conference of Catholic Bishops, 2010).

EXPLANATORY RITES: ANOINTING WITH CHRISM

One of the explanatory rites common to both the ordination of bishops and priests is anointing with sacred chrism. Before considering its particular meaning in each ordination rite, let's first look at the meaning of chrism as a liturgical sign. In addition to the Sacrament of Holy Orders, chrism is also used in the Sacraments of Baptism and Confirmation. It "is a sign that Christians, incorporated by Baptism into the Paschal Mystery of Christ, dying, buried, and rising with him, are sharers in his kingly and prophetic Priesthood and that by Confirmation they receive the spiritual anointing of the Spirit who is given to them."[15] The chrism is made from olive oil or another plant oil mixed with an aromatic substance such as balsam and is consecrated only by a bishop. The *Rite for the Consecration of Chrism* explains the meaning of chrism. The bishop begins by inviting the people to ask God to "bless this oil so that all who are anointed with it may be inwardly transformed and come to share in eternal salvation." Chrism, in all of its sacramental uses, is a sign and means of inner transformation through the working of the Spirit and so contributes to our salvation.

The bishop can choose between two consecratory prayers. Each reveals different aspects of the meaning and power of the chrism.[16] The first prayer asks the Father to "fill it with the power of your Holy Spirit through Christ your Son." This prayer also explains that the name chrism is derived from Christ: "It is from him that Chrism takes its name and with Chrism you have anointed for yourself Priests and kings, Prophets and Martyrs." This prayer emphasizes its use in the Sacrament of Baptism: "Make this Chrism a sign of life and salvation for those who are to be born again in the waters of Baptism."

The second prayer explains how in the Old Testament God "gave your people a glimpse of the power of this holy oil" and then "brought that mystery to perfection in the life of our Lord Jesus Christ." Henceforth, "through the sign of holy Chrism, you dispense your life and love to men." The prayer then asks, "Father, by the power of your love, make this mixture of oil and perfume a sign and source ✝ of your blessing. . . . Above all, Father, we pray that through this sign of

---

15. From the Introduction, *The Rite for the Blessing of Oils and the Consecration of Chrism*, 2.
16. Ibid., 25.

your anointing you will grant increase to your Church until it reaches the eternal glory." Each of the sacraments that includes anointing with chrism gives increase to the Church: Baptism, which incorporates new members into the Body of Christ; Confirmation, which equips believers with the gifts of the Spirit to participate fully in the mission of the Church; and Holy Orders, through which the faithful are instructed in the authentic faith of the apostles and sanctified chiefly through the Eucharist and Penance. This prayer offers a beautiful summary of the power of this liturgical sign: "Let the splendor of holiness shine on the world from every place and thing signed with this oil."

Posture and gesture are also part of this rite. Both bishops and priests are anointed while kneeling before the consecrating bishop, a posture whose meaning we discussed above. Newly ordained bishops are anointed on the head. The anointing is accompanied by the following explanatory words: "May God, who has made you a sharer in the High Priesthood of Christ, himself pour out upon you the oil of mystical anointing and make you fruitful with an abundance of spiritual blessings" (RO, 85). The rite explains that this anointing is a "sign of the Bishop's distinctive share in the Priesthood of Christ" (RO, 26). Newly ordained priests are anointed on the palms their hands. While performing the anointing, the bishop says the following words: "The Lord Jesus Christ, whom the Father anointed with the Holy Spirit and power, guard and preserve you that you may sanctify the Christian people and offer sacrifice to God" (RO, 133). This anointing "symbolizes the Priests' distinctive participation in Christ's Priesthood" (RO, 113). For both bishops and priests, the anointing with chrism is for "a sign of the special anointing of the Holy Spirit who makes their ministry fruitful" (CCC, 1574).

EXPLANATORY RITES: THE ORDINATION OF BISHOPS

There are several explanatory rites specific to the ordination of a bishop: he is given the book of the Gospels, the ring, the miter, and the crosier. Each expresses an important aspect of the episcopal ministry. The ordaining bishop first presents the newly ordained bishop with the Book of the Gospels with these words: "Receive the Gospel and preach the word of God with all patience and sound teaching."

These two gestures involving the Book of the Gospels—holding above the head and then presenting it to the bishop—"illustrate that the faithful preaching of the word of God is the pre-eminent obligation of the office of the Bishop" (RO, 26)

The consecrating bishop next places the ring on the finger of the newly ordained bishop and says, "Receive this ring, the seal of fidelity: adorned with undefiled faith, preserve unblemished the bride of God, the holy Church" (RO, 51). The ring "symbolizes the Bishop's fidelity to the Bride of God, the Church" (RO, 26). Next, the miter is placed on his head, accompanied by these words: "Receive the miter, and may the splendor of holiness shine forth in you, so that when the chief shepherd appears you may deserve to receive from him an unfading crown of glory" (RO, 53). The miter, as the rite explains, is a sign of new bishop's "resolve to pursue holiness" (RO, 26). Finally, the new bishop receives his crosier (pastoral staff), with the following instruction: "Receive the crosier, the sign of your pastoral office: and keep watch over the whole flock in which the Holy Spirit has placed you as Bishop to govern the Church of God" (RO, 26). The crozier "signifies the duty of guiding and governing the Church entrusted to him" (RO, 26).

If the bishop is ordained in his own church (the cathedral, from the Latin *cathedra*, meaning "chair" or "seat"), the principal ordaining Bishop invites him to occupy the *cathedra*, which is the bishop's chair. The bishop's chair—his *cathedra*—is "the sign of his teaching office and pastoral power in the particular Church [diocese], and a sign also of the unity of believers in the faith that the bishop proclaims as shepherd of the Lord's flock" (CB, 42). Only the diocesan bishop, or a bishop he permits to use it, occupies this chair. If the bishop is not ordained in his cathedral, he takes the first place among the concelebrating bishops. The new bishop then sets aside his crosier and receives the fraternal kiss from all the bishops, beginning with the principal ordaining bishop. This fraternal kiss "seals, so to speak, his admittance into the College of Bishops" (RO, 26).

These different explanatory rites reveal several essential aspects of the episcopal office: the book of the Gospels is "the sign of his apostolic mission to proclaim the Word of God"; the ring is a sign "of his fidelity to the Church, the bride of Christ"; the miter signifies his commitment to grow in holiness; and the crosier is a sign of "his office as shepherd of the Lord's flock" (CCC, 1574).

EXPLANATORY RITES: A NOTE ON LITURGICAL VESTMENTS

Immediately following the Prayer of Ordination, the newly ordained priests and deacons are vested in the liturgical vestments proper to their order: stole and chasuble for priests; stole and dalmatic for deacons. Before discussing the meaning of these individual garments, it will be helpful to briefly discuss the theological and sacramental meaning of liturgical vestments in general. For this we must go back to the Garden of Eden, where Adam and Eve, although unclothed, were "not naked but had a wonderful garment in the form of the grace of God."[17] Then came the Fall, and suddenly they were "naked" and so hid themselves from God, for they realized that they were "alienated from and cut off from life-giving and life-preserving communication with the living God."[18] They—and we—experienced "the shame of nakedness, the shame in the face of God, of other people and even oneself."[19] Clothing is an attempt to alleviate this shame, but it always remains "a pale reminder of the lost glory of the spiritual garment of grace."[20]

And then Christ came. He restored to us the spiritual garment of grace, as St. Paul reminded the Galatians: "For all of you who were baptized into Christ have clothed yourselves with Christ" (Gal 3:27). To the Corinthians he explained, "For that which is corruptible must clothe itself with incorruptibility, and that which is mortal must clothe itself with immortality" (1 Cor 15:53). And he exhorted the Ephesians to "put on the new self, created in God's way in righteousness and holiness of truth" (4:24). Liturgical vestments are a sign "on the way to the body's salvation in the risen body of Jesus Christ, which is the new 'house not made with hands, eternal in the heavens.' . . . It is an anticipation of the new clothing, the risen Body of Jesus Christ, that new reality that awaits us."[21]

For the priest as the sacramental sign of Christ, the liturgical vestments which he wears for the celebration of the Mass have an additional

---

17. Michael Kunzler, *The Church's Liturgy*, trans. Placed Murray, OSB, Henry O'Shea, OSB, and Cilian Ó Sé, OSB (London: Continuum, 2001), 128.

18. Ibid.

19. Ibid., 129.

20. Ibid.

21. Ratzinger, *The Spirit of the Liturgy*, 218–219.

significance, for they "make clear that he is not there as a private person, as this or that man, but stands in place of Another—Christ. What is merely private, merely individual, about him should disappear and make way for Christ. . . . It is not he himself who is important, but Christ. It is not he himself whom he is communicating to men, but Christ. He makes himself the instrument of Christ, acting, not from his own resources, but as the messenger, indeed as the presence of another."[22] Liturgical vestments are a sign of this urgent and powerful invitation: "'Put on Christ'—even now be one with him, even now be members of his Body."[23]

EXPLANATORY RITES: THE ORDINATION OF PRIESTS

In addition to anointing on the palms with Chrism, two other explanatory rites accompany the ordination of priests. Prior to the anointing with chrism, the newly ordained priest is vested with stole and chasuble, assisted by some of the priests present. The stole was originally a sort of protective towel or scarf which became a symbol of priestly authority, worn around the neck and falling in vertical strips in front. Current liturgical law stipulates that the stole be worn underneath the chasuble (GIRM, 337). The chasuble began as the outdoor cloak worn by citizens of the Greco-Roman world until the fifth century. It was originally a large square or circular garment with a hole cut in the middle for the wearer's head, hence the name chasuble, from the Latin word *casula*, meaning "little house." St. Isidore of Seville in the seventh century described it as "a garment furnished with a hood, which is a diminutive of *casa*, a cottage, as, like a small cottage or hut, it covers the entire person."[24] By the tenth century the chasuble was seen as a symbol of charity, as St. Ivo of Chartres (d. 1115) explained: "Over all the vestments is superimposed the chasuble . . . which, because it is the common vestment, signifies charity, which is superimposed over all the virtues [see Col 3:12–14], for the other virtues produce nothing

22. Ibid., 216.

23. Ibid., 220.

24. Herbert Thurston, "Chasuble," in *The Catholic Encyclopedia* (New York: Robert Appleton, 1908), 639.

profitable without it."[25] The chasuble is worn over the stole because "in the context of celebrating the Eucharistic Sacrifice, this symbol of charity should surely take precedence over the symbol of authority."[26] Together, the stole and chasuble outwardly manifest "the ministry they will henceforth fulfill in the Liturgy" (RO, 113).

Following the anointing, the bishop presents to the new priests a paten holding the bread and a chalice containing wine mixed with water for the celebration of the Mass. As the bishop hands them to the newly ordained, he says, "Receive the oblation of the holy people, to be offered to God. Understand what you do, imitate what you celebrate, and conform your life to the mystery of the Lord's Cross" (RO, 163). The priest will spend the rest of his earthly life fulfilling this command—understanding the profound spiritual reality of the Holy Sacrifice of the Mass, imitating Christ's gift of himself made present at every Mass, and conforming his life ever more completely to Christ's Paschal Mystery. This rite signifies priests' "duty of presiding at the celebration of the Eucharist and of following Christ crucified" (RO, 113).

The explanatory rites conclude with the bishop giving the newly ordained priest the fraternal kiss and saying, "Peace be with you," which "seals, so to speak, the admittance into their ministry of his new co-workers" (RO, 113). Then the priests present also give the new priest the fraternal kiss, signifying their welcome of "the newly ordained Priests to a shared ministry in their Order" (RO, 113).

EXPLANATORY RITES: THE ORDINATION OF DEACONS

There are three explanatory rites for the ordination of deacons: vesting with the stole and dalmatic, handing on the Book of the Gospels, and the fraternal kiss. Immediately after the prayer of consecration, the new deacon is vested with the stole and dalmatic. The dalmatic is a wide-sleeved garment with slit sides. Deacons originally wore the chasuble, but in the fourth century the dalmatic was worn in Rome by

---

25. Monti, *A Sense of the Sacred*, 169.

26. Peter J. Elliott, *Ceremonies of the Modern Roman Rite: The Eucharist and the Liturgy of the Hours*, rev. ed. (San Francisco: Ignatius, 1995), 46.

deacons and the pope, and so became the official vestment of deacons.[27] The deacon's stole, a symbol of service, was originally worn on the left shoulder over the dalmatic, but since the twelfth century has been worn as a sash from left to right. The dalmatic is the outer garment proper to the deacon (although not strictly required). The dalmatic and stole visibly manifest the liturgical ministry of the deacon.

After he is vested in stole and dalmatic, the new deacon kneels before the bishop, who places the book of the Gospels in his hands and says, "Receive the Gospel of Christ, whose herald you have become. Believe what you read, teach what you believe, and practice what you teach." This action and the explanatory words signify "the office of the Deacon to proclaim the Gospel in liturgical celebrations and to preach the faith of the Church in word and in deed" (RO, 188). The bishop then says, "Peace be with you," and gives him the fraternal kiss. The rite concludes with the other deacons present giving the new deacon the fraternal kiss. The bishop's fraternal kiss "seals, so to speak, the Deacons' admittance into their fraternity." Through their fraternal kiss, the other deacons present "welcome the newly ordained Deacons to a common fraternity in their Order" (RO, 188).

CONCLUSION

Through the Sacrament of Holy Orders the gifts and power of the Holy Spirit are imparted that are appropriate to each of the three degrees: episcopacy, priesthood, and diaconate. This epicletic action is signified by the silent imposition of hands and explained by the words of the Prayer of Ordination specific to each of the degrees of Holy Orders. The meaning of this essential rite is explained and enhanced by other elements such as posture—kneeling, prostration, and standing; vesture—stole, dalmatic, or chasuble; and insignia—the episcopal ring, miter, and crozier, that engage the whole person. The union of the heavenly and earthly liturgy is manifested by the Litany of Supplication. The fraternal character within each degree is signified by the fraternal kiss. Through these mystical rites men are configured in distinctive ways to the one Priesthood of Christ, which "is the love of the heart of Jesus" (St. John Vianney, quoted in CCC, 1589).

---

27. The dalmatic can also be worn by bishops under the chasuble for solemn celebrations: "This applies particularly to the celebration of ordinations, the blessing of an abbot or abbess, and the dedication of a church and an altar" (CB, 56).

Chapter 6

Holy Orders: Living the Sacrament

> Peter, you are the floor, that others
> may walk over you . . . not knowing
> where they go. You guide their steps . . .
> You want to serve their feet that pass
> as rock serves the hooves of sheep.
> The rock is a gigantic temple floor,
> the cross a pasture.

When I wrote these words I was thinking of Peter and the whole reality of the ministerial priesthood, and trying to bring out the profound significance of this liturgical prostration. In lying prostrate on the floor in the form of a cross before one's ordination, in accepting in one's own life—like Peter—the cross of Christ and becoming with the Apostle a "floor" for our brothers and sisters, one finds the ultimate meaning of priestly spirituality.[1]

The priest as a "floor" for his brothers and sisters—in this profound and startling image St. John Paul II expresses the meaning of ordination for the whole of one's life, a total offering of oneself to Christ for others, just as Christ offered himself for us, the Good Shepherd who lays down his life for the sheep (Jn 10:11).

THE INDELIBLE CHARACTER

"The three sacraments of Baptism, Confirmation, and Holy Orders confer, in addition to grace, a sacramental *character* or 'seal' by which the Christian shares in Christ's priesthood and is made a member of the Church according to different states and functions" (CCC, 1121). This sacramental character "cannot be repeated or conferred temporarily" (CCC, 1582). This understanding of a spiritual character or seal comes from the apostle Paul. In two of his letters, St. Paul speaks of Christians being marked with a seal in the context of initiation (see CCC, 698). To

---

1. John Paul II, *Gift and Mystery* (New York: Doubleday, 1996), 45–46.

the Corinthians he wrote that God "has also put his seal upon us and given the Spirit in our hearts as a first installment" (2 Cor 1:22). He reminded the Ephesians that in Christ they "were sealed with the promised holy Spirit" (1:13), and he encouraged them not to "grieve the holy Spirit of God, with which you were sealed for the day of redemption" (4:30).

The Second Vatican Council explained the spiritual character that is imparted through the Sacrament of Holy Orders: "Hence the priesthood of presbyters, while presupposing the sacraments of initiation, is conferred by a special sacrament which, by the anointing of the holy Spirit, puts a special stamp on them and so conforms them to Christ the priest in such a way that they are able to act in the person of Christ the head" (PO, 2).[2] This spiritual character "makes the priest God's own possession. It also conforms his person to Christ and impresses his likeness on him. An imprint is thus etched on personal being, meant to shape all one's actions, which for this very reason carry in themselves a likeness to the Lord's own deeds."[3] The spiritual character imparted through ordination "is first and foremost a relation to God, to the Father, who, first through Christ, then through priests, seeks to reveal himself and bring his own action to bear upon the world."[4] It enables the priest to "serve as Christ's instrument for his Church . . . to act as a representative of Christ, Head of the Church, in his triple office of priest, prophet, and king" (CCC, 1581). The spiritual character is the means by which Christ becomes sacramentally present to the community as the Good Shepherd: "The priestly character imparts the capacity required to so lead the community in the name of Christ that it will be led more and more by the Lord himself."[5]

---

2. "It is true that someone validly ordained can, for grave reasons, be discharged from the obligations and functions linked to ordination, or can be forbidden to exercise them; but he cannot become a layman again in the strict sense, because the character imprinted by ordination is for ever. The vocation and mission received on the day of his ordination mark him permanently" (CCC, 1583).

3. Jean Galot, SJ, *Theology of the Priesthood*, trans. Rev. Roger Balducelli, OSFS, (San Francisco: Ignatius, 1985), 206.

4. Ibid., 204.

5. Ibid., 208. "A priest or bishop who, through grave sin, is no longer in a state of grace, still retains his sacramental character and thus the configuration to Christ the Priest still remains." That he still validly celebrates the sacraments "is an expression of God's mercy, for in this way Christ's faithful are not abandoned to the uncertainty of whether a minister is worthy to perform a sacrament" (Haffner, *The Sacramental Mystery*, 226–227).

Each degree of Holy Orders imparts a specific character. Deacons are marked with a character "which configures them to Christ, who made himself the 'deacon' or servant of all" (CCC, 1570). Through ordination, priests are signed with "a special stamp [that] so conforms them to Christ the priest in such a way that they are able to act in the person of Christ the head" (PO, 2). The sacred character impressed upon bishops through ordination enables them, "in an eminent and visible manner, [to] take the place of Christ himself, teacher, shepherd, and priest, and act as his representative" (CCC, 1558). This spiritual character, then, enables deacons to become the servants of all, priests to act in the person of Christ the head, especially in the sacraments of the Eucharist and Penance, and bishops to take the place of Christ himself and act as his representative.

This, however, raises a question: Are these three separate characters, or one? To assert three different characters could be interpreted as being the result of three separate sacraments, not three degrees of one sacrament, and so increasing the number of sacraments. To assert only one character would obscure the distinctiveness of each Order. "One solution is to propose three characters which are incompletely distinct, rather like interlocking stacking rings which together look like one unit and when separated resemble three rings linked together. In this way, the character of the diaconate forms the basis on which the presbyteral character is added and thereafter sometimes the episcopal character."[6]

This interpretation thus suggests the way for us to proceed in this chapter. We will begin with the meaning of the diaconate for life, then add to it the priesthood, and conclude with the episcopacy. The ordination rite for each degree conveys the meaning for the whole of life, so we will look first at each rite as well as the propers (prayers and preface) from the Ritual Mass for Ordination. We will then supplement this information with other sources such as the *Catechism of the Catholic Church* and documents from the Second Vatican Council.

THE DEACON

One of the preparatory rites for ordination is the questioning of the candidate by the bishop. These questions address the obligations that

---

6. Haffner, *The Sacramental Mystery*, 226.

each candidate for Holy Orders freely accepts, and they delineate the duties specific to each Order.[7] Each of the promises, as we will see, is the work of a lifetime. The first question put to candidates for the diaconate is this: "Do you resolve to be consecrated for the Church's ministry by the laying on of my hands and the gift of the Holy Spirit?" Consecration for the Church's ministry is not a job with set hours, but a vocation, an availability to the prompting of the Spirit, an openness to others, just as Jesus was always open to the needs and suffering of others. The candidate is next asked if he will "discharge the office of Deacon with humble charity in order to assist the priestly Order and to benefit the Christian people." What is important is not so much fulfilling a task as the attitude with which it is done—"humble charity"—in imitation of Christ's own humility (cf. Phil 2:6–11).

The third question concerns the deacon's responsibility to teach the faith: "Do you resolve to hold fast to the mystery of faith with a clear conscience, as the Apostle urges, and to proclaim this faith in word and deed according to the Gospel and the Church's tradition?" The reference to the Apostle's urging is to the First Letter to Timothy: "deacons must be dignified . . . holding fast to the mystery of faith with a clear conscience" (3:8–9). This imposes on the deacon a lifelong commitment to deepen their understanding of the faith of the Church, lived and taught with sincerity and integrity. He is being made a steward of the faith entrusted by the Lord to his Church, and it is that faith he is to teach, not his own opinions.

If the candidate is unmarried, he is next asked if he is resolved "to remain celibate as a sign of your dedication to Christ the Lord for the sake of the Kingdom of Heaven, in the service of God and man?" [8] The discipline of celibacy for unmarried permanent deacons "is placed in the context of the *undivided heart*, that is within the context of a nuptial, exclusive, permanent and total choice of the unique and greatest Love; service of the Church can count on a total availability; the proclamation

---

7. All of these questions used in the rite are from the *Rite of Ordination of Deacons*, no. 228, in the *Roman Pontifical*.

8. The Second Vatican Council restored the permanent diaconate, which is open to single and married men. Those ordained to the permanent diaconate are not candidates for the priesthood, but candidates for the priesthood are first ordained to the diaconate, which is often referred to as the transitional diaconate, since it is a step toward ordination to the priesthood. This question is put to unmarried candidates for the transitional and permanent diaconate.

of the Kingdom is supported by the courageous witness of those who have left even those things most dear to them for the sake of the Kingdom."[9] As this passage from the *Directory* indicates, celibacy for the unmarried permanent deacon gives a specific orientation to the whole of his life, since it is a free, permanent and total choice to serve God with an undivided heart to make oneself available to God and his people as Christ himself did.

Those preparing for ordination to the priesthood make their promise of celibacy at their diaconal ordination—this promise is not repeated in the ordination of priests. The Second Vatican Council explained the meaning of celibacy for the priest: "There are many ways in which celibacy is in harmony with the priesthood. . . . They more readily join themselves to [Christ] with undivided heart and dedicate themselves more freely in him and through him to the service of God and of men and women. They are less encumbered in their service of his kingdom and of the task of heavenly regeneration. In this way they become better fitted for a broader acceptance of fatherhood in Christ" (PO, 16). By living with joy and fruitfulness their promise of celibacy, priests "recall that mystical marriage, established by God and destined to be fully revealed in the future, by which the church holds Christ as her only spouse. Moreover they are made a living sign of that world to come, already present through faith and charity, a world in which the children of the resurrection neither marry nor be given in marriage (see Lk 20:35–36)" (PO, 16). Celibacy for the priest, then, is "a sign of God's love for this world and of the undivided love of the priest for God and for God's people" (PDV, 29).

The deacon-elect is next questioned about his commitment "to maintain and deepen the spirit of prayer that is proper to your way of life and, in keeping with this spirit and what is required of you, to celebrate faithfully the Liturgy of the Hours with and for the People of God and indeed for the whole world." The Liturgy of the Hours, also known as the divine office, is "the public prayer of the Church" (SC, 98) in obedience to St. Paul's exhortation to the Thessalonians, "Pray without ceasing" (1 Thes 5:17). It is comprised of psalms, Old and New Testament canticles (e.g., Is 42:10–16 and Eph 1:3–10), readings from Sacred Scripture, intercessions, and readings from the saints, especially

---

9. Congregation for Catholic Education and Congregation for Clergy, *Directory for the Ministry and Life of Permanent Deacons,* chapter 2, n. 36.

the Church Fathers. It consists of five daily "offices": the Office of Readings, Morning Prayer, Daytime Prayer, Evening Prayer, and Night Prayer. "It is truly the voice of a bride addressing her bridegroom; it is the very prayer that Christ himself, together with his Body, addresses to the Father" (SC, 84). It, along with the Eucharist, is one of the cornerstones of the deacon's prayer life, supplemented by other forms of prayer, both official devotions such as the Rosary or the Chaplet of Divine Mercy and personal forms of mental or contemplative prayer. In the United States, permanent deacons are required to pray two offices daily, Morning Prayer and Evening Prayer.[10]

This is followed by the most comprehensive question: "Do you resolve to conform your way of life always to the example of Christ, of whose Body and Blood you are a minister at the altar?" Several of the prayers for the Ritual Mass for the Ordination of Deacons express a similar idea. The opening prayer (Collect) asks that the candidates "be effective in action, gentle in ministry, and constant in prayer" (RM). The Prayer over the Offerings asks God to "grant that, offering ourselves as a spiritual sacrifice, we may be filled with a spirit of humility and zeal" (RM). Finally, the Solemn Blessing at the conclusion of the Mass includes these petitions: "May he, who has entrusted you with preaching the Gospel of Christ, help you, as you live according to his word, to be its sincere and fervent witnesses," and "May he . . . make you imitators of his Son, Jesus Christ, and ministers of unity and peace in the world" (RM). This transformed way of life is beautifully summarized by the Second Vatican Council. In the *Dogmatic Constitution on the Church (Lumen Gentium)*, it urges deacons to "recall the admonition of St. Polycarp [martyred in 155]: 'Let them be merciful, and zealous, and let them walk according to the truth of the Lord, who became the servant of all'" (LG, 29).

The final promise concerns the deacon's relationship to his bishop: "Do you promise respect and obedience to me and my successors?" The model for the deacon's obedience to his bishop is Christ, who "humbled

---

10. "Permanent deacons are required to include as part of their daily prayer those parts of the Liturgy of the Hours known as Morning and Evening Prayer. Permanent deacons are obliged to pray for the universal Church. Whenever possible, they should lead these prayers with the community to whom they have been assigned to minister" (United States Conference of Catholic Bishops, *National Directory for the Formation, Ministry, and Life of Permanent Deacons in the United States* [Washington DC: USCCB Publishing, 2005], 40).

himself, becoming obedient to death, even death on a cross" (Phil 2:8; DMLPD, 8). "He shall conform his own obedience in listening (Heb 10:5ff.; Jn 4:34) and in radical availability (cf. Lk 9:54ff. and 10:1ff.) to the obedience of Christ. He shall therefore dedicate himself to working in complete conformity with the will of the Father and devote himself to the Church by means of complete availability" (DMLPD, 8). St. John Paul II elaborated on the nature of this obedience, noting that "an outlook of contestation or of opposition to authority" is incompatible with the diaconate, which "can only be conferred on those who believe in the value of the pastoral mission of bishops and priests and in the assistance of the Holy Spirit who helps them in their activities and in the decisions they take. . . . The service of the deacon is directed to a particular Christian community for which he should develop a profound attachment both to its mission and divine institution." [11]

The bishop's final exhortation to the newly ordained deacon concisely expresses his new way of life: "Receive the Gospel of Christ, whose herald you have become. Believe what you read, teach what you believe, and practice what you teach" (RO, 238). The deacon is a herald of the Gospel not only by his words, but equally if not even more by his actions and life. He is an incarnation of the Gospel that he proclaims.

THE PRIEST

We will now examine the meaning of ordination for the life of priests. As with the diaconate, we will begin by looking at the Promises of the Elect, bearing in mind the promises they made when they were ordained deacons. [12] The priest-elect is first asked about his readiness "to discharge without fail the office of Priesthood in the presbyteral rank, as a worthy fellow worker with the Order of Bishops in caring for the Lord's flock." The model for priests is "the love of the good shepherd to give their lives for their sheep (see Jn 10:11)" (PO, 13). As leaders and examples for their community, they should "cultivate the form of asceticism suited to a pastor of souls, renouncing their own convenience, seeking not their own good, but that of the many, that they may be saved (see 1 Cor 10:33), always making further progress towards a more

---

11. Catechesis of John Paul II at the General Audience of October 20, 1993, n. 2, *Insegnamenti*, XVI, 2, (1993), p. 1055.

12. All of the quoted questions are from the *Rite of Ordination of Priests*, n. 152.

perfect fulfillment of their pastoral work and, where the need arises, prepared to break new ground in pastoral methods under the guidance of the Spirit of love who breathes where he wills (see Jn 3:8)" (PO, 13). To paraphrase St. John Bosco, "the priest is a priest at the altar; he is a priest in the confessional; he is a priest at the school; he is a priest on the street; indeed, he is a priest everywhere."[13]

The candidate next promises "to exercise the ministry of the word worthily and wisely, preaching the Gospel and teaching the Catholic faith." This promise commits the priest to a lifelong intimate relationship with the Word of God. "The priest," wrote St. John Paul II, "is first of all a minister of the word of God" (PDV, 26). This reality applies first to his encounter with Christ in his Word. He "needs to approach the word with a docile and prayerful heart so that it may deeply penetrate his thoughts and feelings and bring about a new outlook in him—'the mind of Christ' (1 Cor 2:16)—such that his words and his choices and attitudes may become ever more a reflection, a proclamation and a witness to the Gospel" (PDV, 26). His proclamation of the Gospel goes beyond his homilies and catechetical presentations—it is proclaimed as well by his choices and attitudes. Pope Francis reiterated the importance of this in his exhortation *The Joy of the Gospel* (*Evangelii Gaudium*): "Whoever wants to preach must be the first to let the word of God move him deeply and become incarnate in his daily life. In this way preaching will consist in that activity, so intense and fruitful, which is 'communicating to others what one has contemplated'" (EG, 150, quoting Aquinas). The Collect for the ordination of priests and deacons beautifully expresses this ministry of the word, asking that those to be ordained would be "ardent yet gentle heralds of your Gospel" (RM, For the Ordination of Deacons and Priests in the Same Celebration).

The candidate is next asked if he is resolved "to celebrate faithfully and reverently . . . the mysteries of Christ, especially the Sacrifice of the Eucharist and the Sacrament of Penance, for the glory of God and the sanctification of the Christian people" (*Rite of Ordination of Priests*, 152). This promise places special emphasis on priests as ministers of the Eucharist and of the Sacrament of Penance. In their celebration of the Mass, in which they act in the person of Christ, "they are invited to imitate what they handle, so that as they celebrate the mystery of the

---

13. Congregation for the Clergy, *The Priest, Pastor and Leader of the Parish Community* (Boston: Pauline, 2002), 11.

Lord's death they may take care to mortify their members from vices and concupiscences" (PO, 13). In addition, in their celebration of the Eucharistic Sacrifice "they daily offer themselves completely to God, and by being nourished with Christ's body they share in the charity of him who gives himself as food to the faithful" (PO, 13).

This charity also finds expression in their celebration of the Sacrament of Penance. Priests "are united with the intention and the charity of Christ" in their administration of the all of the sacraments, but "in a special way when they show themselves to be always available to administer the sacrament of Penance whenever it is reasonably requested" (PO, 13). To fulfill this promise, priests are encouraged to "acquire the knowledge and prudence necessary for this task by serious study, guided by the teaching authority of the Church and especially by fervent prayer to God. Discernment of spirits is a deep knowledge of God's action in the hearts of men; it is a gift of the Spirit as well as the fruit of charity" (RP, 10a). Priests are also urged to avail themselves regularly of the Sacrament of Penance, "becoming themselves witnesses of God's mercy toward sinners" (PDV, 26). The priests' celebration of the sacraments, then, commits them to the ongoing intellectual formation as well as constant pursuit of holiness and conformity to the availability and charity of Christ. This is expressed in the Solemn Blessing for the Ritual Mass for Ordination: "May he make you servants and witnesses in the world to divine charity and truth and faithful ministers of reconciliation" (RM, For the Ordination of Several Priests).

Next, the candidate accepts the responsibility to "implore with us God's mercy upon the people entrusted to your care by observing the command to pray without ceasing." This promise recalls the promise the candidate made at his diaconal ordination "to maintain and deepen the spirit of prayer" and "to celebrate faithfully the Liturgy of the Hours with and for the People of God and indeed for the whole world." The priest-elect, then, has already formed the habit of faithfully praying the Liturgy of the Hours. In praying the Liturgy of the Hours, priests "lend their voice to the church which perseveres in prayer in the name of the whole human race, in union with Christ who 'always lives to make intercession for them' (Heb 7:25)" (PO, 13).

The fifth promise is "to be united more closely every day to Christ the High Priest, who offered himself for us to the Father as a pure Sacrifice, and with him to consecrate yourself/yourselves to God for the salvation of all" (RO, 152). The fulfillment of this promise is intimately connected to the priest's personal holiness, for "while it is possible for God's grace to carry out the work of salvation through unworthy ministers, yet God ordinarily prefers to show his wonders through those who are more responsive to the impulse and guidance of the holy Spirit and who, because of their intimate union with Christ and their holiness of life, are able to say with St. Paul: 'It is no longer I who live, but Christ who lives in me' (Gal 2:20)" (PO, 12). For this reason, the Church urges priests to pursue holiness "by the use of all suitable means commended by the church" so that they may be ever more docile and effective representatives of Christ for the salvation of all (PO, 12).

The final promise is "respect and obedience" to the bishop and his successors, a promise already made by the candidate at his ordination to the diaconate. The model, as we noted above, is Christ who was "obedient to death, even death on a cross" (Phil 2:8) and who "learned obedience from what he suffered" (Heb 5:8). It is with good reason, then, "that obedience to the Father is the very heart of the Priesthood of Christ" (DMLP, 61). Furthermore, the priest's obedience to his legitimate superiors becomes an ever-greater source of joy and freedom when "continually deepened in the presence of God in prayer" (DMLP, 61). A specific petition in the Collect for the Ritual Mass for Ordination conveys the comprehensive meaning of this virtue: "grant a persevering obedience to your will . . . so that by their ministry and life they may gain glory for you in Christ."

At the conclusion of his ordination to the diaconate, the priest-elect was charged by the bishop to "believe what you read, teach what you believe, and practice what you teach." As a newly-ordained priest, he receives an additional charge. He kneels before the bishop, who places in his hands a paten with bread and chalice with wine mixed with water and says, "Receive the oblation of the holy people, to be offered to God. Understand what you do, imitate what you celebrate, and conform your life to the mystery of the Lord's Cross" (*Rite of Ordination of Priests*, 163). The mystery of the Lord's Cross is the mystery of self-giving love, a love that goes "to the end" (Jn 13:1). According to St. John Chrysostom, this "means that he left nothing undone that one who greatly loved should do."[14] This is the pastoral charity that the priest is called to manifest in his life.

> ### Promises
>
> Summarize the promises made by candidates for the diaconate and priesthood. Are any promises repeated?

THE BISHOP

We now come to the meaning of episcopal ordination, again recalling the image of stacking and interlocking rings as a way to understand the relationship of character imprinted by episcopal ordination to the characters already conferred through diaconal and priestly ordination. Just as the sacramental characters build on one another, so too do the Promises of the Elect.

The first promise of the bishop-elect is to "resolve by the grace of the Holy Spirit to discharge until death the office entrusted to us by the Apostles, which we are about to pass on to you by the laying on of our hands"[15] The office conferred on the bishop is humbling in its magnitude, for "bishops, eminently and visibly, take the place of Christ himself, teacher, shepherd and priest, and act in his person" (LG, 21). Its meaning for the whole of the bishop's life is beautifully expressed by the prayers for the Ritual Mass for the Ordination of a Bishop. May he "direct by word and example the people entrusted to his care" (RM, For the Ordination of a Bishop, Collect); "grant, we pray, that by his holiness of life he may everywhere prove to be a true witness to Christ" (ibid.); and "may he . . . be endowed, by your gift, with apostolic virtues" (ibid., Prayer over the Offerings). His in a preeminent way is a ministry of authority and example, for he must "everywhere prove to be a true witness to Christ," and so in a preeminent way he needs the gracious gift of "apostolic virtues" (ibid., Collect).

The next two promises of the bishop-elect concern his teaching office. First, he is to "preach the Gospel of Christ with constancy and fidelity." According to the Second Vatican Council, among the duties of

---

14. Joel C. Elowsky, ed., *John 11–21*, Ancient Christian Commentary on Scripture (Downers Grove, IL: InterVarsity, 2007), 83.

15. All of the quoted questions are from the *Rite of Ordination of a Bishop*, 40.

a bishop "preaching the Gospel has pride of place" (LG, 25). Second, he promises "to guard the deposit of faith, entire and incorrupt, as handed down by the Apostles preserved in the Church everywhere and at all times." For the bishops are "authentic teachers of the faith, that is, teachers endowed with the authority of Christ" who preach the faith to the flock entrusted to their care, "the faith which is to be believed and applied in practice" (LG, 25). Enlightened by the Holy Spirit, "they cause that faith to radiate; . . . they make it bear fruit and they vigilantly ward off whatever errors threaten their flock" (LG, 25).

The bishop-elect is next asked if he is resolved "to build up the body of Christ, his Church, and to remain in the unity of that Body together with the Order of Bishops under the authority of the successor of Saint Peter the Apostle." Through ordination bishops are constituted members of the college of bishops in union with the Pope, just as "in accordance with the Lord's decree, St. Peter and the other apostles constitute one apostolic college" (LG, 22). This is expressed sacramentally "by the Church's ancient practice which calls for several bishops to participate in the consecration of a new bishop" (CCC, 1559). In addition to the flock entrusted to his care, each bishop shares with his brother bishops "the apostolic mission of the Church"—his authority and responsibility are simultaneously local and universal (CCC, 1560). For this reason, the bishop-elect is next asked if he will "render obedience faithfully to the successor of the blessed Apostle Peter." This communion with the Pope is vital, for the "body of bishops has no authority . . . other than . . . in union with the Roman Pontiff, Peter's successor, as its head" (LG, 22). This college of bishops united under the Pope manifests both the diversity and the unity of the Church: diversity by virtue of its worldwide membership, unity "in so far as it is assembled under one head" (LG, 22).

The next three questions focus on the bishop-elect's care for the flock. Will he "guide the holy People of God in the way of salvation as a devoted father and sustain them with the help of [his] fellow ministers, the Priests and Deacons?" Will he, "for the sake of the Lord's name, be welcoming and merciful to the poor, to strangers, and to all who are in need?" Will he "resolve as a good shepherd to seek out the sheep who stray and gather them into the Lord's fold?" These questions use two images to describe the bishop's relationship to those entrusted to him: he is to be a "devoted father" and a "good shepherd." A father's sense of responsibility for his children never ceases, nor does a shepherd's care for his flock. At the same time, the questions convey the extent of the bishop's flock—the holy People of God, the poor, strangers, all who are in need, and those who have strayed. One understands why the Church has provided bishops with priests and deacons to assist them. The bishop can take as his own the words of St. Paul: "Who is weak, and I am not weak? Who is led to sin, and I am not indignant?" (2 Cor 11:29).

Finally, the bishop-elect promises, "with the help of God . . . to pray without ceasing to almighty God for the holy people and to carry out the office of High Priest without reproach." The bishop-elect for the third time (first as a deacon-elect and again as a candidate for priesthood) promises to pray unceasingly for the people of God. Because he "represents Christ in an eminent and conspicuous way and is the high priest of his flock, . . . he should, then, be the first of all the members of his Church in offering prayer" (GILH, 28). He prays the Liturgy of the Hours "always . . . in the name of the Church and on behalf of the Church entrusted to him" (GILH, 28). He carries out the office of High Priest as the representative before God "to offer gifts and sacrifices for sins," for he is "the principal dispense[r] of the mysteries of God" (CD, 15). He is "'the steward of the grace of the supreme priesthood,' above all in the Eucharist, which he himself offers, or ensures that it is offered, and by which the church continues to live and grow" (LG, 26). His authority is great because his responsibilities are vast.

As we saw with deacons and priests, so too with bishops—there can be no separation between their public ministry and their way of life: "by the example of their way of life they should exercise a powerful influence for good on those over whom they are placed, by abstaining from all wrongdoing in their conduct, and doing their utmost, with the help of the Lord, to make their conduct even more admirable, so that together with the flock entrusted to them, they may attain eternal life" (LG, 26). The Solemn Blessing at the conclusion of the Mass for the Ordination of Bishops, at which the newly ordained bishop normally presides, includes this petition: "make me pleasing to you in the fulfillment of my duties" (RM). His ordination is for the salvation of others—but also for his own salvation.

THE GRACE OF THE HOLY SPIRIT

There are two effects of the Sacrament of Holy Orders. The first is the sacramental character, which we discussed at the beginning of this chapter. The second is a specific grace of the Holy Spirit, which configures men "to Christ as Priest, Teacher, and Pastor, of whom the ordained is made a minister" (CCC, 1585). To deacons is bestowed the grace of the Spirit for "the service (*diakonia*) of the liturgy, of the Gospel, and of works of charity" (CCC, 1588). To priests is bestowed the grace of Holy Spirit for the worthy celebration of the sacraments, especially the Eucharist. To the bishop is given a grace of strength "to proclaim the Gospel to all, to be the model for his flock, to go before it on the way of sanctification by identifying himself in the Eucharist with Christ the priest and victim, not fearing to give his life for his sheep" (CCC, 1586). To each Order is given the grace of the Spirit to enable the recipients to live out their ministry in every aspect of their life.

CONCLUSION

There are several texts that are common to the ordination of deacons, priests, and bishops, and they provide a fitting conclusion to this chapter. The Preface for Priesthood of Christ and the Ministry of Priests used at ordinations for all three degrees describes the absolute commitment the Orders entails:

> As they give up their lives for you
> and for the salvation of their brothers and sisters,
> they strive to be conformed to the image of Christ himself
> and offer you a constant witness of faith and love. (RM)

And Eucharistic Prayer I (the Roman Canon), includes this petition when used at the Ritual Mass for Holy Orders:

> In your mercy, keep safe your gifts in me,
> so that what I have received by divine commission
> I may fulfill by divine assistance. (RM)

The Sacrament of Holy Orders is begun by God and brought to completion by Him.

PART III

The Sacrament of Matrimony

The Bible begins and ends with wedding imagery. "Sacred Scripture begins with the creation of man and woman in the image and likeness of God and concludes with a vision of 'the wedding-feast of the Lamb'" (CCC, 1602). This encapsulates the richness and importance of the Sacrament of Matrimony: it is rooted in the original design of creation, it manifests the mystery of God who is three and one, and it is a sign of Christ's relationship with his Church.

In chapter 7 we will present a brief overview of the sacrament before looking at marriage within the context of creation and as an image and likeness of the Trinity, which is a loving communion of persons. Since marriage is a covenant, we will also examine God's covenantal relationship with Israel and his promise of a new covenant in Jeremiah 31. Finally we will consider several key Old Testament figures and passages: Isaac and Rebekah, Tobiah and Sarah, the Song of Songs, the virtuous wife in Proverbs 31, and God's promise through Jeremiah of a new covenant.

Next, in chapter 8, we will explore the liturgical signs that comprise the Sacrament of Matrimony. These signs include the presence of the minister and congregation as signs of Christ, Head and Body, as well as the exchange of consent by the spouses, the exchange of rings, and the Nuptial Blessing. We also look at two adaptations from Hispanic culture, the *lazo* (lasso) and *arras* (coins).

We will conclude by reflecting on the meaning of this sacrament for the whole of one's life. In chapter 9 we will look at the marital bond effected by the sacrament and the unique participation in the life of the Trinity brought about by the sacrament. We will consider the unity of marriage, the gift of new life, the responsibility of educating children, and the missionary vocation of marriage. These transformative aspects of the sacrament reflect both the mystery of the Trinity and Christ's nuptial covenant with his body, the Church.

Chapter 7

Matrimony: Old Testament Roots

IN THE BEGINNING

When the Pharisees asked Jesus about the legality of a man divorcing his wife "for any cause," he replied, "from the beginning of creation, 'God made them male and female. For this reason a man shall leave his father and mother [and be joined to his wife], and the two shall become one flesh'. So they are no longer two but one flesh. Therefore, what God has joined together, no human being must separate" (Mk 10:6–9). Christ himself teaches that marriage was part of the original design of creation, specifically in the creation and union of man and woman, a truth reaffirmed by the Second Vatican Council: "God himself is the author of marriage" (GS, 48).

Since it is part of creation that God proclaimed "good," marriage manifests and contributes to this inherent goodness. "The well-being of the individual person and of both human and christian society is closely bound up with the healthy state of the community of marriage and the family" (GS, 47). Although the "force and strength" of marriage come from creation, "for the Christian faithful it is also raised to a higher dignity, since it is numbered among the Sacraments of the new covenant" (OCM, 1). This elevation of nature by grace is affirmed in the Ritual Mass for Marriage: "For you willed that the human race, created by the gift of your goodness, should be raised to such high dignity that in the union of husband and wife you might bestow a true image of your love" (OCM, 201).

The Sacrament of Marriage is a *covenant* "by which a man and a woman establish between themselves a partnership of the whole of life" (CCC, 1601). This partnership exists for the good of the spouses and the generation and education of children—the two "ends" of marriage. It contributes to the good of the spouses by a distinctive sharing in the life of Christ: "The content of participation in Christ's life is also specific: conjugal love involves a totality, in which all the elements of the person enter—appeal of the body and instinct, power of feeling and affectivity, aspiration of the spirit and of will" (FC, 13). The generation and education of children is also a participation in the love of the Trinity, for it requires a wholehearted cooperation "with the love of the Creator and Savior," who enriches the spouses with "a spirit of sacrifice" by which they glorify God and pursue Christian perfection (OCM, 10). By embracing these two ends of marriage, spouses "help one another to become holy" and contribute to the building up of the Kingdom of God (OCM, 8). Christian marriage both signifies and participates in "the mystery of unity and fruitful love between Christ and the Church" (OCM, 8). In the words of the liturgy, "in the wedding covenant you foreshadow the Sacrament of Christ and his Church" (Collect B, OCM, 188).

Christian marriage possesses four goods and requirements: unity, fidelity, indissolubility, and openness to fertility. These four are intrinsically related, for the unity of marriage is "a deeply personal unity, the unity that, beyond union in one flesh, leads to forming one heart and soul; it demands indissolubility and faithfulness in definitive mutual giving; and it is open to fertility" (FC, 13). They cannot be separated. They mirror in a specific way the mystery of the Trinity, which is an indissoluble unity of Persons whose reciprocal and fruitful love gives rise to the immense richness and beauty of the world. They are also intrinsic aspects of the two ends of marriage, for "the intimate union of marriage, as a mutual giving of two persons, and the good of the children demand total fidelity from the spouses and require an unbreakable unity between them" (GS, 48). The goods and requirements of marriage, which are "the normal characteristics of all natural conjugal love," receive through the celebration of the sacrament "a new significance which not only purifies and strengthens them, but raises them to the extent of making them the expression of specifically Christian values" (FC, 13).

As with all sacraments, the Sacrament of Marriage "signifies and communicates grace" (CCC, 1617), the divine life and power of God. This grace perfects the spouses' human love, strengthens their unity, and sanctifies them on the way to eternal life (CCC, 1662). The sacrament "gives the spouses the grace to love each other with the love with which Christ has loved his Church" (CCC, 1661). In addition, through the sacrament God establishes between the spouses an indissoluble bond that "is a reality . . . and gives rise to covenant guaranteed by God's fidelity" (CCC, 1640). "Their belonging to each other is the real representation, by means of the sacramental sign, of the very relationship of Christ with the Church" (FC, 13). This communion of man and woman "represents the mystery of Christ's incarnation and the mystery of His covenant" (FC, 13). Like the Sacrament of Holy Orders, the Sacrament of Marriage "introduces one into an ecclesial *order*, and creates rights and duties in the Church between the spouses and towards their children" (CCC, 1631).

Marriage, a sign of Christ's self-giving love for his bride the Church, is intrinsically related to the Eucharist, and so the Sacrament of Marriage should normally be celebrated within the Mass.[1] St. Paul affirmed the spousal character of both sacraments: "Husbands, love your wives, even as Christ loved the church and handed himself over for her to sanctify her, cleansing her by the bath of water and the word, that he might present to himself the church in splendor, without spot or wrinkle or any such thing, that she might be holy and without blemish" (Eph 5:25–27). St. John Paul II elaborated on the relationship between these two sacraments, calling the Eucharist "the very source of Christian marriage," because it "represents Christ's covenant of love with the Church, sealed with His blood on the Cross (Jn 19:34)" (FC, 57). The Eucharist, the sacrament of charity, is a re-presentation "of Christ's sacrifice of love for the Church," his Paschal Mystery, and so becomes for the faithful "a fountain of charity" (FC, 57). The spouses "seal their consent to give themselves to each other through the offering of their own lives by uniting it to the offering of Christ for his Church made present in the Eucharistic sacrifice, and by receiving the Eucharist so that, communicating in the same Body and the same Blood of Christ, they may form but 'one body' in Christ" (CCC, 1621). Furthermore, as God blesses the couple with children, the Eucharist becomes for the Christian family "the foundation and soul of its 'communion' and its 'mission'", becoming one body and so revealing and sharing "in the wider unity of the Church" (FC, 57). Christ's Body given up for us and his Blood shed for us is "a never-ending source of missionary and apostolic dynamism for the Christian family" (FC, 57).

---

1. For pastoral reasons, however, the pastor may propose that Marriage be celebrated without Mass (OCM, 29). There is another rite for marriage between a Catholic and a catechumen or a non-Christian (OCM, 118–143).

The celebration of the Sacrament of Marriage begins with the Introductory Rites, for which there are two options. In the first form, the priest greets the couple at the door of the church and they together process to the altar. In the second form, the priest meets the couple at the place prepared for them in the church or goes to his chair. He then speaks to the couple and those present in order "to dispose them inwardly for the celebration of Marriage" (OCM, 52). The Mass continues with the Liturgy of the Word. The homily, based on the biblical readings, should "expound the mystery of Christian Marriage, the dignity of conjugal love, the grace of the Sacrament, and the responsibilities of married people" (OCM, 57). The Celebration of Marriage follows the homily. The couple is first questioned "about their freedom of choice, fidelity to each other, and the acceptance and upbringing of children" (OCM, 60). They next declare their consent, which is "the indispensable element that 'makes the marriage.' If consent is lacking there is no marriage" (CCC, 1626). The priest then receives their consent. This is followed by the Blessing and Giving of Rings and the Universal Prayer. The Mass then continues with the Liturgy of the Eucharist. After the Our Father, the priest gives the Nuptial Blessing. The Mass may conclude with a Solemn Blessing.

IN THE ORDER OF CREATION

As we noted above, the Old Testament roots of marriage go back to Genesis 1, to the creation of the world. On the sixth day of creation "God said: Let us make human beings in our image, after our likeness. . . . God created mankind in his image; in the image of God he created them; male and female he created them. . . . And so it happened. God looked at everything he had made, and found it very good" (Gn 1:26–27, 30–31). The Scriptures further teach that man and woman were created for each other. "The LORD God said: It is not good for the man to be alone. I will make a helper suited to him" (Gn 2:18). When she is brought to the man, he said "This one, at last, is bone of my bones and flesh of my flesh. . . . That is why a man leaves his father and mother and clings to his wife, and the two of them become one body" (Gn 2:23–24). The creation of human beings, male and female, is presented as the culmination of creation, and the plants and animals are created for them and given to them (Gn 1:28–30). This is why the

Church teaches that "the vocation to marriage is written in the very nature of man and woman as they came from the hand of the Creator" (CCC, 1603), a truth affirmed by the Marriage liturgy: "O God, who in creating the human race willed that man and wife should be one" (Collect, OCM, 189).

The fact that Marriage is an inseparable aspect of creation makes it unique among the sacraments. As St. John Paul II explains: "The sacrament of Matrimony has this specific element that distinguishes it from all the other sacraments: it is the sacrament of something that was part of the very economy of creation; it is the very conjugal covenant instituted by the Creator 'in the beginning'" (FC, 68). Man and woman were created in the image and likeness of God, who is a loving communion of persons. Indeed, love is "the fundamental and innate vocation of every human being" (CCC, 1604). Married love "becomes an image of the absolute and unfailing love with which God loves man" (CCC, 1604).

COVENANT

Marriage is a covenant, an image rooted in the Old Testament. The *Catechism* defines a covenant as "a solemn agreement between human beings or between God and a human being involving mutual commitments or guarantees" (CCC, Glossary). The word "testament" is a synonym for "covenant," so the Old Testament is an account of God's covenantal relationship with his Chosen People in preparation for the coming of Christ. The New Testament is the revelation of God's new covenant in Christ, established "through his own sacrificial death and Resurrection" (ibid.). The Mass is a re-presentation of Christ's new covenant with the Church and a reaffirmation by the faithful of their acceptance of and commitment to that covenant.

The Old Testament prophets used the image of faithful and exclusive married love to describe God's covenant with Israel. Through the prophet Hosea God promised Israel, "I will make a covenant for them on that day. . . . I will betroth you to me forever: I will betroth you to me with justice and with judgment, with loyalty and with compassion; I will betroth you to me with fidelity, and you shall know the LORD" (2:20–22). The prophet Jeremiah rebuked Judah and Israel, describing their idol worship as infidelity, prostitution and adultery: "With her

[Israel's] casual prostitution, she polluted the land, committing adultery with stone and wood. In spite of all this, Judah, the traitor, her sister, did not return to me wholeheartedly, but insincerely" (Jer 3:9–10). We find the same image in the prophet Isaiah: "For your husband is your Maker; / the LORD of hosts is his name, / Your redeemer, the Holy One of Israel, / called God of all the earth. / The LORD calls you back, / like a wife forsaken and grieved in spirit, / A wife married in youth and then cast off, / says your God. / For a brief moment I abandoned you, / but with great tenderness I will take you back" (Is 54:5–7).

The *Catechism* explains that through these prophecies God "prepared the Chosen People's conscience for a deepened understanding of the unity and indissolubility of marriage" (CCC, 1611). St. John Paul II saw these Old Testament passages as foreshadowing marital love: "Their bond of love becomes the image and the symbol of the covenant which unites God and His people (Hos 2:21; Jer 3:6–13; Is 54)" (FC, 12). "The nuptial covenant between God and his people Israel had prepared the way for the new and everlasting covenant in which the Son of God, by becoming incarnate and giving his life, has united to himself in a certain way all mankind saved by him, thus preparing for 'the wedding-feast of the Lamb'" (CCC, 1612).

Digging into the *Catechism of the Catholic Church*

Read the description of the stages of revelation, CCC, 54–73, noting especially the importance of covenant. What did each of the covenants signify?

OLD TESTAMENT READINGS

The Lectionary provides a number of Old Testament readings for the celebration of the Sacrament of Marriage. As we will see, they lay the foundation for important aspects of the sacrament. They affirm that God is not only the author of the sacrament, but also of each marriage, to which he commits himself in covenant fidelity. We will also discover precursors of the Nuptial Blessing and the free consent of the spouses. Finally, we will encounter texts that reveal the two ends of marriage, the good of the spouses and the gift of children.

We have already considered the first two Old Testament options, the accounts of the creation of human beings in Genesis 1 and Genesis 2. A third option, Genesis 24:48–51, 58–67, describes the marriage of Isaac and Rebekah. Abraham, not wanting his son to marry a Canaanite, sends his servant to his own land and kindred to get a wife for Isaac. Arriving at the city of Nahor in the evening, the servant waits at the well outside of the city and prays that God would show him who is to be Isaac's wife. Then he sees Rebekah, helps her draw water for her camels, and gives her a gold nose ring and two gold bracelets. In his conversation with her he discovers that she is of the house of Abraham's brother, for which he blesses God: "the LORD has led me straight to the house of my master's brother" (Gn 24:27).

The servant dines with the family of Laban, Rebekah's brother, but before he eats he tells them why he has come. The selection for the celebration of marriage picks up the story at this point. The servant asks Laban if he agrees to give his sister to Isaac. Laban acknowledges that "this thing comes from the LORD; we can say nothing to you either for or against it" (Gn 24:50). When the servant prepares to leave, Laban and his mother call Rebekah and ask her, "Will you go with this man?" She answers, "I will" (Gn 24:58). As she is departing, they bless her: "Sister, may you grow / into thousands of myriads; / And may your descendants gain possession / of the gates of their enemies!" (Gn 24:60).

This passage reveals several important aspects of the Sacrament of Marriage. First, God is the true author of each marriage. Just as Laban acknowledged that it is God who brought Isaac and Rebekah together, so the rite also affirms that it is God who brings the couple together, asking him to strengthen those "whom you have brought to their wedding day" (Eucharistic Prayer II, OCM, 203) so that "the union you have created may be kept safe by your assistance" (OCM, 192). This Old Testament passage also illustrates the importance of the spouses freely offering their consent as Rebekah did when questioned by her family. Finally, the blessing Rebekah receives from her family foreshadows the Nuptial Blessing and the gift of children as one of the ends of marriage.

Another Old Testament reading is the description of Tobiah's marriage to Sarah in Tobit 7:6–14. Sarah has already been given in marriage seven times, and all have died in the bridal chamber. Raphael tells Tobiah how to ward off the demon who killed Sarah's previous husbands (6:16–18). He then assures Tobiah that Sarah has been chosen for him "before the world existed" and that he will save her and they will have children together. Tobiah goes to the house of his kinsman Raguel and asks to marry his daughter Sarah. Raguel, joyous at discovering that Tobiah is Tobit's son, readily assents, confident that it is the will of God, who will look after both of them. He asks God's prosperity, mercy, and peace upon them both. He then takes Sarah's hand and gives her to Tobiah saying, "According to the decree written in the Book of Moses I give her to be your wife. Take her and bring her safely to your father. And may the God of heaven grant both of you a safe journey in peace!" (7:12). In this passage we see God's goodness and fidelity. The spouses are brought together by the grace and will of God, who sustains and protects them in their life together.

Tobit 8:4b–8 is another Old Testament option, and it continues the story of Tobiah and Sarah. It records Tobiah's prayer in the bedroom. Tobiah begins by blessing God. He then recalls God's creation of Adam and Eve, "his helper and support" (8:6). He next professes, "not with lust, but with fidelity I take this kinswoman as my wife" (8:7). Finally, he invokes God's blessing on his marriage to Sarah: "Send down your mercy on me and on her, and grant that we may grow old together. Bless us with children" (8:7). This passage also reaffirms marriage as part of creation and the gift of conjugal unity. Tobiah's petition for mercy anticipates themes found in the Nuptial Blessing, specifically the blessing of children ("may they be blessed with children," OCM, 74), and a long life together ("grant that, reaching at last together the fullness of years for which they . . . " OCM, 74; "after a happy old age," OCM, 139, 209). These readings from Tobit "bear moving witness to an elevated sense of marriage and to the fidelity and tenderness of spouses" (CCC, 1611).

Another Old Testament option comes from the Canticle of Canticles (2:8–10, 14, 16a; 8:6–7a), also known as the Song of Songs, "an exquisite collection of love lyrics, arranged to tell a dramatic tale of mutual desire and courtship."[2] It has been read as a profound description of God's love for his people, Christ's love for his Church. These verses speak especially of marriage as ordained for the good of the spouses: "My lover speaks and says to me, 'Arise, my friend, my beauti-

---

2. "Introduction to the Song of Songs," in *New American Bible*, rev. ed., St. Joseph medium size ed. (Totowa, NJ: Catholic Book Publishing, 2011), 775.

ful one, and come!" (2:10). It affirms their unity and indissolubility: "My lover belongs to me and I to him" (2:16a). It praises the strength of love, "strong as Death" (8:6), for "deep waters cannot quench love, nor rivers sweep it away" (8:7a). And it alludes to the marriage bond itself: "Set me as a seal upon your heart, as a seal upon your arm" (8:6). "Tradition has always seen in the *Song of Solomon* a unique expression of human love, insofar as it is a reflection of God's love—a love 'strong as death' that 'many waters cannot quench'" (CCC, 1611).

The Church also includes two Old Testament descriptions of the virtuous wife, Proverbs 31:10–13, 19-20, 30–31 and Sirach 26:1–4, 13–16. Proverbs 31 praises the "woman of worth" who works diligently (v. 19), cares for the poor and needy (v. 20), and fears the Lord. She knows that charm and beauty are ephemeral. "Her husband trusts her judgment" and "her deeds praise her at the city gates" (vv. 11, 31). A good wife, says Sirach, is "bestowed upon him who fears the Lord" (26:3). She is thoughtful, gracious and self-disciplined, modest and chaste (vv. 13–15). "The beauty of a good wife in her well-ordered home" is like "the sun rising in the Lord's heavens" (v. 16). The virtues listed in Proverbs and Sirach are invoked in the Nuptial Blessing: "let her always follow the example of those holy women whose praises are sung in the Scriptures" (OCM, 74). The analogy of a good wife in her home with the rising sun is also alluded to: "Graciously crown with your blessings your daughter N., so that, by being a good wife (and mother), she may bring warmth to her home with a love that is pure and adorn it with welcoming graciousness" (OCM, 207).

The final Old Testament passage we will consider is Jeremiah 31:31–32a, 33–34a, the promise of "a new covenant with the house of Israel and house of Judah" (31:31). This new covenant is the law of God written up their hearts, God's promise that "I will be their God, and they shall be my people" (Jer 31:33). It embraces all—"Everyone, from least to greatest, shall know me" (31:34). It is the definitive promise of God's forgiveness: he will "no longer remember their sin" (Jer 31:34). This passage is quoted twice in the New Testament Letter to the Hebrews as being fulfilled by Christ. The passage is first quoted to support the assertion that Christ "has obtained so much more excellent a ministry as he is mediator of a better covenant, enacted on better promises" (8:6). The prophecy of the new covenant, argues the writer, is a declaration that the previous covenant is now obsolete (8:13). The writer then specifically identifies this new covenant with Christ's Paschal Mystery. Christ, the eternal high priest, "offered one sacrifice for sins, and took his seat forever at the right hand of God. . . . For by one offering he has made perfect forever those who are being consecrated" (10:12, 14). He supports this by quoting Jeremiah 31:33, which he calls the testimony of the Holy Spirit "to us" (10:15). Jeremiah's prophecy of a new covenant, a prophecy fulfilled by Christ, deepens our understanding of the covenant of marriage. The Eucharist is the sacrament of Christ's covenant, the re-presentation of "the new and eternal covenant" of which marriage is a sign and from which marriage draws its power. "Christian marriage . . . becomes an efficacious sign, the sacrament of the covenant of Christ and the Church" (CCC, 1617).

The texts for marriage explore the profound relationship between the covenantal dimension of these two sacraments. Consider, for example, this Preface: "in him [Christ] you have made a new covenant with your people, so that, as you have redeemed man and woman by the mystery of Christ's Death and Resurrection, so in Christ you might make them partakers of divine nature and joint heirs with him of heavenly glory. In the union of husband and wife you give a sign of Christ's loving gift of grace, so that the Sacrament we celebrate might draw us back more deeply into the wondrous design of your love" (OCM, 200). Marriage is a sign of Christ's new covenant, his "loving gift of grace", that draws not just the spouses but all the faithful "more deeply into the wondrous design" of the love of the Blessed Trinity. God's loving design is also recalled in one of the Nuptial Blessings: "O God, who, to reveal the great design you formed in your love, willed that the love of spouses for each other should foreshadow the covenant you graciously made with your people, so that, by the fulfillment of the sacramental sign, the mystical marriage of Christ with his Church, might become manifest in the union of husband and wife among your faithful" (OCM, 207). It is the loving will of the Creator that marital love should prefigure God's gracious covenant with his people and make visible "the mystical marriage of Christ with his Church."

> ## Old Testament Roots
>
> Review the Old Testament readings for marriage. Which readings speak of the following aspects of marriage?
>
> 1. The couple brought together by God
>
> 2. The gift of children
>
> 3. The consent of the spouses
>
> 4. God's fidelity to the couple
>
> 5. Human love as a sign of divine love
>
> 6. The relationship between Marriage and Eucharist

CONCLUSION

A study of the Old Testament roots of the Sacrament of Marriage reveals a rich foundation for understanding the sacrament. It is unique among the sacraments in being part of the original plan of creation. It enriches our understanding of what it means to be created in the image and likeness of God. It reveals that God is not only the author of marriage, but also the author and guarantor of each marriage in covenant fidelity. We have also seen the biblical origins for the Nuptial Blessing. Finally, it shows how the sacrament is both a sign of and a participation in the love of the Trinity.

Chapter 8

Marriage: Signs and Symbols of the Sacrament

INTRODUCTION

The Sacrament of Matrimony is woven from a diversity of liturgical signs. It employs gestures such as joining hands and hands raised in blessing, postures such as standing and kneeling, and processions. Rings express important human and spiritual realities, as do cultural symbols such as coins (*arras*) and the lasso (*lazo*). Holy water is used a sign of God's blessing. Together these signs communicate to the couple "the saving and sanctifying action of Christ" (CCC, 1189). In this chapter we will examine these signs in detail, for "when minds are enlightened and hearts are enkindled, signs begin to 'speak'" (MND, 14).

The celebration of the Sacrament of Matrimony within the Mass consists of two parts: Introductory Rites that take place at the beginning of Mass, and the Celebration of Matrimony following the Homily. This is followed by the Liturgy of the Eucharist and concludes with a Solemn Blessing over the spouses. In the Introductory Rites, the priest greets the couple and speaks briefly about the Sacrament of Marriage. The Mass continues with the Liturgy of the Word. The Homily, based on the biblical readings, explains "the mystery of Christian Marriage, the dignity of conjugal love, the grace of the Sacrament, and the responsibilities of married people" (OCM, 57). The Celebration of Marriage follows. The couple is first questioned about the essential elements of Marriage: freely entering into the covenant of Marriage, fidelity and indissolubility, and openness to children. They next declare their consent, which the priest receives in the name of the Church. This is followed by the Blessing and Giving of Rings and the Universal Prayer. The Mass then continues with the Liturgy of the Eucharist. After the Our Father, the priest gives the Nuptial Blessing. The Mass may conclude with a Solemn Blessing. Figure 8.1 summarizes the celebration of Marriage.

Figure 8.1 Structure of the Sacrament

Introductory Rites
(greeted at church entrance or at the place prepared for them in the church)
Liturgy of the Word: Readings and Homily
Celebration of Marriage (all standing)
Questions
Consent (join hands)
Blessing of Rings (sign of cross, holy water)
Exchange of Rings (hymn or canticle)
Universal Prayer
Liturgy of the Eucharist
Nuptial Blessing
(epiclesis, hands extended)
(after Lord's Prayer, embolism is omitted)
Sign of Peace
Solemn Blessing
(epicletic, hands extended)

THE INTRODUCTORY RITES

There are two options for the Introductory Rites. In the first option, the priest, vested in white or another festive color, meets couple at the door of the church and "warmly greets them, showing that the Church shares in their joy" (OCM, 45). In the second form, the priest meets the couple at the place prepared for them in the church or goes to his chair. Once all the participants are in their places, the priest speaks to the couple and those present in order "to dispose them inwardly for the celebration of Marriage" (OCM, 52). The rite provides two models, stipulating that the priest may use "these or similar words." For the couple, "this is a moment of unique importance," for on this day they intend to establish between themselves "a lifelong partnership" (OCM, 53). The assembly is urged to support the couple with prayers, affection, and friendship and to "listen attentively with them to the word that God speaks to us today" (OCM, 52). All present are reminded that they gather as part of the universal Church and with her join their prayers for the couple, God's servants, "that he lovingly accept them, bless them, and make them always one" (OCM, 52). This may conclude with special petitions for the couple: "May the Lord hear you on this your joyful day. May he send you help from heaven and protect you. May he grant you your hearts' desire and fulfill every one of your prayers" (OCM, 53).

These introductory rites are significant for the language of sign that they employ. The priest greets the couple at the door to show that the Church shares their joy. The procession to the altar signifies that Marriage is a sign of Christ's self-giving love for the Church. The instructions to those gathered emphasize that the celebration of this sacrament, as with all the sacraments, is not a private celebration but a celebration of the whole Church, the Body of Christ, Head and members. Finally, the rites include a simple catechesis on the sacrament to enable all present to participate more fully in the celebration.

INTRODUCING THE CELEBRATION OF MARRIAGE

Following the Homily, all stand for the celebration of Marriage. This is another example of the importance of posture in the liturgy. Standing is "the basic posture of an Easter people lifted up to greet their risen Lord" (IOM, 29), the posture "of those who have risen with Christ and seek the things that are above."[1] It also expresses a readiness for action. It is a particularly apt posture for celebrating the Sacrament of Marriage, which is a sign of Christ's self-giving, covenantal love for the Church, a sacrament which itself "becomes an efficacious sign, the sacrament of the covenant of Christ and the Church" (CCC, 1617).

The priest begins by addressing the couple. He may use the remarks in the rite "or similar words." In the model introduction, the priest begins by summarizing why the couple has come to the Church, "so that in the presence of the Church's minister and the community your intention to enter into Marriage may be strengthened by the Lord with a sacred seal" (OCM, 59). He then briefly characterizes the meaning of the Sacrament of Marriage, explaining that Christ "enriches and

---

1. United States Conference of Catholic Bishops, *Praying with Body, Mind, and Voice* (Washington, DC: United States Conference of Catholic Bishops, 2010).

strengthens those he has already consecrated by Holy Baptism, that they may be faithful to each other for ever and assume all the responsibilities of married life." He also asks that their intention to commit themselves to Marriage "may be strengthened by the Lord with a sacred seal" (OCM, 59).

CONSENT

The mutual consent of the spouses is "the indispensable element that 'makes the marriage'" (CCC, 1626). Through this consent, which is irrevocable, the spouses "freely give themselves to each other and accept each other" (OCM, 2). This consent establishes the Marriage covenant—without it, there is no Marriage. For this reason, the Catholic Church teaches that "the spouses as ministers of Christ's grace mutually confer upon each other the sacrament of Matrimony by expressing their consent before the Church" (CCC, 1623).

This consent must be a free act of the will by each spouse, neither coerced nor imposed through fear (CCC, 1628). The priest questions the couple about their freedom to enter into Marriage and their understanding of the two goods of Marriage. He first asks the couple if they have "come here to enter into Marriage without coercion, freely and wholeheartedly?" He next asks if they are prepared "to love and honor each other for as long as you both shall live?" Finally, he asks if they are "prepared to accept children lovingly from God and to bring them up according to the law of Christ and his Church?"[2] (OCM, 60). These are the concrete signs which establish the necessary freedom to enter into marriage and to fulfill the two ends of marriage, the good of the spouses and the generation and education of children.

The priest then invites the couple to join their right hands and declare their consent "before God and his Church" (OCM, 61). The act of joining hands is found in Tobit, when Raguel took his daughter Sarah "by the hand and gave her to Tobiah" (Tb 7:12; cf. Monti, 213). The bridegroom says to his bride, "I, N., take you, N., to be my wife. I promise to be faithful to you, in good times and in bad, in sickness and in health, to love you and to honor you all the days of my life" (OCM, 62). The bride then says, "I, N., take you, N., to be my husband," followed by the same promise. The rite provides the option of obtaining consent through

---

2. This question can be omitted if circumstances such as the age of the couple suggest it.

questioning: "N., do you take N. to be your wife/husband? Do you promise to be faithful . . ." (OCM, 63), to which the other answers, "I do."

The priest, whose presence is a visible sign of "the fact that marriage is an ecclesial reality" (CCC, 1630), receives their consent "in the name of the Church" (CCC, 1630). The rite provides two formulas for the Reception of Consent: "May the Lord in his kindness strengthen the consent you have declared before the Church, and graciously bring to fulfillment his blessing within you. What God joins together, let no one put asunder"; or "May the God of Abraham, the God of Isaac, the God of Jacob, the God who joined together our first parents in paradise, strengthen and bless in Christ the consent you have declared before the Church, so that what God joins together, no one may put asunder" (OCM, 64). The priest then says to the assembly, "Let us bless the Lord," to which they reply "Thanks be to God", or another similar response. This participation by the assembly further signifies the ecclesial dimension of Marriage.

BLESSING AND GIVING OF RINGS

The exchange and Reception of Consent, the essential element of the sacrament, is followed by the Blessing and Giving of Rings. The custom of wedding rings was taken over from Roman betrothal rings at an early date. The earliest Christian blessing of the rings comes from the marriage of England's King Edilwulf to Judith of France in 856. The blessing explained the meaning of this liturgical sign: "Receive the ring, the sign of faithfulness and love and the bond of conjugal union, inasmuch as man must not separate those God has joined."[3]

The custom of placing the ring on the fourth finger goes back to Saint Isidore of Seville (d. 636), who "attributed it to the belief that there was a vein in the fourth finger that ran directly to the heart," a belief traceable to the Roman author Pliny the Elder (d. 79).[4] In the Middle Ages the placing of the ring was accompanied by a Trinitarian formula. According to a late fifteenth-century liturgical text, "the priest should place the ring on the bridegroom's thumb, saying, *In the name of the Father.* And afterward on the index finger, and he should say, *And of*

---

3. James Monti, *A Sense of the Sacred: Roman Catholic Worship in the Middle Ages* (San Francisco: Ignatius, 2012), 215.

4. Ibid., 216.

the Son. Then on the middle finger; and he should say, *And of the Holy Spirit.* Then he should leave the ring on the bridegroom's fourth finger, saying, *Amen.*"[5]

The rite begins with the priest blessing the rings. It provides three different formulas:

- "May the Lord bless ✚ these rings, which you will give each other as a sign of love and fidelity." (OCM, 66)
- "Bless, O Lord, these rings, which we bless ✚ in your name, so that those who wear them . . . " (OCM, 194)
- "Bless ✚ and sanctify your servants in their love, O Lord, and let these rings, a sign of their faithfulness, remind them of their love for one another." (OCM, 195)

The blessing includes the Sign of the Cross, and the priest may sprinkle the rings with holy water.

The blessing of the rings is an example of a *sacramental*. Sacramentals are sacred signs instituted by the Church "which bear a resemblance to the sacraments" (CCC, 1667). The effects which they signify "are obtained through the intercession of the Church" (CCC, 1667). They differ from sacraments in three important ways.

1. The Seven Sacraments have been instituted by Christ, while sacramentals are instituted by the Church.
2. The sacraments are effective whenever they are celebrated using the rite approved by the Church by the proper minister who, in doing so, intends what the Church intends.[6] Sacramentals are effective through the prayer of the Church.
3. Sacraments confer grace whenever they are celebrated "in accordance with the intention of the Church" (CCC, 1128), while sacramentals "prepare us to receive grace and dispose us to cooperate with it" (CCC, 1670) and "sanctify different circumstances of life" (CCC, 1677).

---

5. Ibid., 217.

6. "This is the meaning of the Church's affirmation that the sacraments act *ex opere operato* (literally: 'by the very fact of the action's being performed'), i.e., by virtue of the saving work of Christ, accomplished once for all. . . . From the moment that a sacrament is celebrated in accordance with the intention of the Church, the power of Christ and his Spirit acts in and through it, independently of the personal holiness of the minister" (CCC, 1128).

Sacramentals usually include a prayer and a sign such as the Sign of the Cross or the sprinkling of holy water. Examples of sacramentals include blessings of persons, places, meals, and things, as well as exorcisms.

The use of holy water is an ancient tradition. Water was used in purifying sprinklings in French monasteries in the early Middle Ages. Beginning in the eighth century, this developed into a blessing of water and sprinkling before the Eucharist. It was adopted by parish churches and incorporated into the Missal of 1570. The meaning of the sprinkling changed from purification to a recalling of Baptism, as the Rite for Blessing and Sprinkling of Water in the current Missal explains: "Dear brethren, let us humbly beseech the Lord our God to bless this water he has created, which will be sprinkled on us as a memorial of our Baptism" (Appendix II).

The current rite retains the traditional symbolism discussed above. The rings are first and foremost "a sign of love and fidelity" (OCM, 66 and 67A) and a reminder "of their love for one another" (195). One of the blessing formulas asks that those who wear the rings "may remain entirely faithful to each other, abide in peace and in your will, and live always in mutual charity" (194). The Trinitarian symbolism discussed above (although not the accompanying gesture) is preserved in the current rite. The words said by each spouse when placing the ring conclude with the Trinitarian formula, "In the name of the Father, and of the Son, and of the Holy Spirit" (67A).

> ## Digging into the Catechism
>
> Read the section in the *Catechism of the Catholic Church* on sacramentals, 1667–1679.

Nuptial Blessing: The Epiclesis

The celebration now continues with the Liturgy of the Eucharist. Following the Our Father, the prayer "Deliver us, Lord, we pray . . . " is omitted, and the priest invokes God's blessing upon the couple through the Nuptial Blessing, which is never omitted. There are numerous Old Testament examples of blessings given to the bride or the spouses. As we noted in chapter 2, the invocation of the Holy Spirit—the epiclesis—is one of the central elements of every sacrament. The epiclesis of the Sacrament of Marriage is the Nuptial Blessing, through which "the spouses receive the Holy Spirit as the communion of the love of Christ and the Church" (CCC, 1624). This gift of the Holy Spirit is active in three ways in the Sacrament of Marriage:

- first, it "is the seal of their covenant";
- second, it is "the ever available source of their love"; and
- third, it is "the strength to renew their fidelity" (CCC, 1624).

The gift of the Holy Spirit specific to the Sacrament of Marriage strengthens and sustains the couple throughout their life together.

For the Nuptial Blessing the couple either approaches the altar or remains in their place and kneels. The priest then invites the assembly to pray. The invitation summarizes the meaning of the Nuptial Blessing. One form asks that the Lord would "mercifully pour out the blessing of his grace and make of one heart in love those he has joined by a holy covenant" (RM, Nuptial Blessing A; OCM, 73). A second form asks that the spouses "may always be bound together by love for one another" (RM, Nuptial Blessing B; OCM, 206). A third form asks for God's blessing, "that in his kindness he may favor with his help those on whom he has bestowed the Sacrament of Matrimony" (Nuptial Blessing C; OCM, 208). The Holy Spirit is invoked to unite in love those "now married in Christ" (OCM, 73). The Holy Spirit now bestowed will be a constant source of help throughout the couple's life together.

> ### Posture
>
> Review the different meanings kneeling has in the liturgy (see chapter 2). Which meaning(s) does it have as the posture for the Nuptial Blessing?

The priest then extends his hands over the bride and bridegroom in the epicletic gesture and proclaims the Nuptial Blessing. The present rite offers three forms of the Nuptial Blessing (referred to here as A, B, and C, following the *Roman Missal* [OCM, 74, 207–209]). This blessing consists of several distinct sections, which are summarized in figure 8.2.

Figure 8.2 Structure of the Nuptial Blessing

Nuptial Blessing Form A	*Nuptial Blessing Form B*	*Nuptial Blessing Form C*
Summary of Creation	Summary of Creation	Summary of Creation
Sign of Christ's Covenant with Church	Sign of Christ's Covenant with Church	Petition for Each Spouse
Invocation of Holy Spirit	Invocation of Holy Spirit	Invocation of Holy Spirit
Petitions for Each Spouse	Petitions for the Couple	Petitions for the Couple
Petition for Final Salvation	Petition for Final Salvation	Petition for Final Salvation

All three Nuptial Blessings begin by placing Marriage in the plan of creation. The fullest treatment is found in Form A: "O God, who by your mighty power created all things out of nothing, and, when you had set in place the beginnings of the universe, formed man and woman in your own image, making the woman an inseparable helpmate to the man, that they might no longer be two, but one flesh, and taught that what you were pleased to make one must never be divided." This opening section teaches God's creation of the world from nothing, the creation of man and woman in God's image, and the unity and indissolubility of their union.

The next section describes Marriage as an image of Christ's covenant with the Church. "O God, who, to reveal the great design you formed in your love, willed that the love of the spouses for each other should foreshadow the covenant you graciously made with your people, so that, by the fulfillment of the sacramental sign, the mystical marriage of Christ with his Church might become manifest in the union of husband and wife among your faithful" (Form B). This section concisely weaves together three covenant themes: God's covenant with his people Israel, the covenant of marriage, and Christ's covenant with his bride, the Church. The covenant of marriage was foreshadowed by God's covenant with his people, and through the sacramental sign the spouses manifest "the mystical marriage of Christ with his Church" (OCM, 207).

This is followed by the epiclesis proper—the invocation of the Holy Spirit upon the couple. Each Nuptial Blessing reveals a different aspect of the gift of the Holy Spirit. Form A emphasizes the gift of the Spirit as the source of marital fidelity: "Send down upon them the grace of the Holy Spirit and pour your love into their hearts, that they may remain faithful in the Marriage covenant" (OCM, 74). Form B refers to the power of the Spirit: "Graciously stretch out your right hand over these your servants (N. and N.), we pray, and pour into their hearts the power of the Holy Spirit" (OCM, 207). It also makes explicit reference to the epicletic gesture, asking God to graciously stretch out his right hand over the couple. Form C asks for the gift of divine love: "may the power of your Holy Spirit set their hearts aflame from on high." Fidelity, power, and hearts aflame with the love of the Trinity are specific gifts bestowed on the couple by the Holy Spirit.

The next sections of the Nuptial Blessing invoke blessings on each spouse and on them as a couple. These will be discussed in the following chapter, since they reveal important aspects of the meaning of the sacrament for the whole of the couple's life together. The Nuptial Blessing concludes with petitions for the final salvation of the couple. Form A asks that "they may come to the life of the blessed in the Kingdom of Heaven." Form B asks that they "may one day have the joy of taking part in your great banquet in heaven." The petition in Form C is the simplest: "may they come to the Kingdom of Heaven."

ADAPTATIONS: *ARRAS* AND *LAZO*

All of the sacraments permit certain adaptations, which are outlined in the last section of the Introduction found at the beginning of each of the ritual books. For example, the *Order for the Celebration of Marriage* permits, "in keeping with local customs, the crowning of the bride or the veiling of the spouses" following the giving of rings (OCM, 41.5). The joining of hands and the Blessing and Giving of Rings can be omitted or replaced if these "are incompatible with the culture of the people" (OCM, 41.6). Finally, "elements from the traditions and culture of particular peoples" can be adopted after careful and prudent consideration (OCM, 41.7). An example of this is the option approved by the

American bishops of including two elements from the Hispanic tradition: the Exchange of Coins (*Arras*) and the Blessing and Placing of the Lasso or Veil.

The Exchange of Coins, or *Arras*, normally takes place after the Blessing and Giving of Rings. The rite begins with the Blessing of the *Arras* (Coins):

> Bless, ✚ O Lord, these *arras*
> that N. and N. will give to each other
> and pour over them the abundance of your good gifts.[7]

The bridegroom gives coins to his bride, who receives them by placing her hands below her husband's hands. In handing over the coins, the bridegroom says, "N., receive these *arras* as a pledge of God's blessing and a sign of the good gifts we will share" (OCM, 67B). The wife receives the arras and then gives them to the husband and says, 'N, receive these arras as a pledge of God's blessing and a sign of the good gifts we will share" (OCM, 67B). As these words indicate, the *Arras* concludes the wedding contract. The *arras* are a sign of God's blessing and also a sign "that the couple will share everything mutually."[8] According to custom, thirteen coins are often used as a sign of prosperity[9] as well as "the presence of Christ and his disciples."[10]

Depending on local custom, "the rite of blessing and imposition of the *lazo* (wedding garland) of the veil may take place before the Nuptial Blessing" (OCM, 71B). The words of the blessing express the meaning of the *lazo*: "Bless, ✚ O Lord, this *lazo* (or: this veil), / a symbol of the indissoluble union / that N. and N. have established from this day forward / before you and with your help."[11] "The *lazo* (or the veil) is held by two family members or friends and is placed over the shoulders of the newly married couple" (OCM, 71B). The *lazo* signifies the unity and indissolubility of Marriage and the grace—"your help"—that God grants through the sacrament. The *lazo* is removed at the conclusion of the Nuptial Blessing.

---

7. OCM, 67B.

8. James L. Empereur and Eduardo Fernandez, *La Vida Sacra: Contemporary Hispanic Sacramental Theology* (Lanham, MD: Rowman & Littlefield, 2006), 156.

9. Mark R. Francis and Arturo J. Perez-Rodriguez, *Primero Dios: Hispanic Liturgical Resource* (Chicago: Liturgy Training Publications, 2007), 104.

10. Empereur, *La Vida Sacra*, 156.

11. OCM, 71B.

SOLEMN BLESSING

The final liturgical sign is the blessing of the couple at the conclusion of Mass. The Ritual Mass for the Celebration of Marriage includes several Solemn Blessing formulas. The solemn blessing is inserted after the dialogue, "The Lord be with you. R/: And with your spirit," indicated by the invitation given by the priest or deacon, "Bow down for the blessing." It consists of three separate invocations; after each invocation the assembly responds, "Amen." The priest says the blessing with his hands extended over the people, the gesture that accompanies an epiclesis. It concludes with the general formula, "And may the blessing of almighty God, the Father, and the Son, ✚ and the Holy Spirit, come down on you and remain with you for ever. R/: Amen," and the Dismissal.

The tripartite structure is modeled on the threefold blessing God instructed Aaron to give the Israelites:

> The LORD bless you and keep you!
> The LORD let his face shine upon you, and be gracious to you!
> The LORD look upon you kindly and give you peace!" (Nm 6:24–26)

In addition to the solemn blessings for the Celebration of Marriage, the *Roman Missal* contains a large number of solemn blessings for other occasions. There are twenty different solemn blessings for Celebrations in the Different Liturgical Times, such as Advent, the Beginning of the Year, Easter Time, The Holy Spirit, and six options for Ordinary Time. There are four solemn blessings for Celebrations of the Saints, one for the Dedication of a Church, and one for Celebrations for the Dead. Several Ritual Masses also include optional solemn blessings: Confirmation, Anointing of the Sick, Holy Orders, the Blessing of an Abbot or Abbess, the Consecration of Virgins, Religious Profession. Appropriate solemn blessings can be used not only at the end of Mass, but also to conclude liturgies of the word and the Liturgy of the Hours.[12]

The solemn blessings are "undoubtedly a great acquisition, because they add appropriate aspects to the general formula of blessing and interpret them as well."[13] This is certainly true of the three options

---

12. Johannes H. Emminghaus, *The Eucharist: Essence, Form, Celebration*, trans. Linda M. Maloney, rev. and ed. Theodor Mass-Ewerd (Collegeville, MN: The Liturgical Press, 1997), 213.

13. Ibid., 214.

provided for the Celebration of Marriage. The first option (Form A)[14] includes petitions for mutual love and the peace of Christ; blessing in children, comfort in friendship, and peace with all; and effective witness to the charity of Christ. The second option, Form B in the *Roman Missal*, is explicitly Trinitarian in structure, asking that God the Father would grant joy and bless the couple in their children, that the Only Begotten Son of God would support them with his compassion in good and bad times, and that the Holy Spirit of God would always pour forth his love into their hearts.

The third option is a threefold petition to Christ, invoking different aspects of the relationship between his love for the Church and marital love. The first petition is that Christ would bless the couple and their loved ones just as he blessed the marriage at Cana, for "the Church attaches great importance to Jesus' presence at the wedding at Cana. She sees in it the confirmation of the goodness of marriage and the proclamation that thenceforth marriage will be an efficacious sign of Christ's presence" (CCC, 1613). The interpretation by St. Maximus of Turin is a good example: "The Son of God went to the wedding so that marriage, which had been instituted by his own authority, might be sanctified by his blessed presence."[15] Christ is next asked to pour his love into the hearts of the bride and groom as he "loved the Church to the end," a reference to John's description of Christ's love for his disciples as he prepared to wash their feet: "He loved his own in the world and he loved them to the end" (13:1). Finally, he is asked to enable the couple to "await with joy the blessed hope to come" as they bear "witness to faith in his Resurrection."

These solemn blessings offer a concise catechesis on the Sacrament of Marriage. The first summarizes the ends of Marriage and its missionary dimension. The second emphasizes the sacrament as the work of and communion with the Trinity. And the third option highlights the sacrament as a sign of Christ's relationship with the Church.

---

14. Form A is discussed in more detail in the following chapter.

15. Joel C. Elowsky, ed., *John 1–10,* Ancient Christian Commentary on Scripture (Downers Grove, IL: Inter Varsity Press Academic, 2007), 90.

CONCLUSION

The Sacrament of Marriage employs a rich variety of signs and symbols to make present "the saving and sanctifying action of Christ" (CCC, 1189). Gestures such as joining hands and hands raised in blessing signify powerful spiritual realities. Postures such as standing and kneeling signify interior dispositions of humility and readiness. The sacramental of holy water signifies the holiness of marital unity symbolized by the rings. Cultural adaptations like the *arras* and *lazo* reveal how the Church incorporates into the liturgy elements of human culture, "conferring on them the dignity of signs of grace, of the new creation in Jesus Christ" (CCC, 1149). And the rich use of blessings signify the power of the Spirit sent from Christ to communicate the Father's love, for "blessing is a divine and life-giving action, the source of which is the Father; his blessing is both word and gift" (CCC, 1078). Together they reveal and make present the life of the Trinity and Christ's love for his Church.

Chapter 9

Living the Sacrament of Matrimony

INTRODUCTION

Marriage is a sign of the Trinity, a mysterious communion of persons that is at the same time and without contradiction an indissoluble unity. The Spirit is given to the spouses through the Sacrament of Matrimony to enable them to manifest ever more authentically this Trinitarian reality of a loving communion of persons and to continually deepen their unity and to enrich it through the gift of children. Marriage is also a sign of Christ's faithful love for his Church, and the sacrament bestows on the spouses a new relationship with Christ through the Spirit to live out their spousal love with the same faithfulness and indissolubility that characterizes Christ's love for the Church. Finally, the grace of the sacrament equips the Christian family to participate in the missionary activity of the Church, in union with Christ who was sent by the Father (Jn 3:17; 5:36, 38: 6:29, 38; 10:36; 11:42; 17:3; 20:21).

The Sacrament of Marriage strengthens and consecrates the spouses "for the duties and dignity of their state" (CCC, 1638). Vatican Council II taught that marital love combines the human and divine and permeates the spouses' whole lives so that, "penetrated with the spirit of Christ . . . their whole life is suffused with faith, hope and charity" (GS, 48). The Sacrament of Matrimony, wrote St. John Paul II, confers on the spouses "the grace and moral obligation of transforming their whole lives into a 'spiritual sacrifice'" (FC, 56). This is why he taught that the Sacrament of Marriage initiates "in a true and proper sense a journey towards salvation" (FC, 68). The two effects of marriage—the marital bond and the grace of the Sacrament of Marriage—are the foundation for this sacramental transformation.

MARITAL BOND

God himself establishes the marital bond "in such a way that a marriage concluded and consummated between baptized persons can never be dissolved" (CCC, 1640). This bond, which results from the free human act of the spouses, is a reality and cannot be revoked. It gives rise to the marital covenant that is "guaranteed by God's fidelity" (CCC, 1640). Rooted in the covenantal love of God, it is perpetual and exclusive. This means that the marital bond is not some sacred "thing"; rather, it brings the spouses into a new and perpetual relationship with the Blessed Trinity, which springs from Christ's covenant with his bride, the Church.

St. Paul explains the relationship between the married couple on the one hand, and Christ and the Church on the other, in his letter to the Ephesians. After exhorting husbands to love their wives as Christ loved the Church (Eph 5:25–30), he writes, "For this reason a man shall leave his father and his mother and be joined to his wife, and the two shall become one flesh. This is a great mystery, but I speak in reference to Christ and the church" (Eph 5:31–32). It is of great significance that in this explanation, the mystery of Christ and the Church precedes the mystery of Christian marriage. "What the sacrament adds is . . . the love of Christ and his Church in which the husband and wife will share. The mystery comes first; it both reveals the divine meaning of the union of the spouses and makes that meaning a reality in them."[1] What takes place through the sacrament is a mysterious identity between sacramental sign and spiritual reality: "In a sacramental marriage there is a personal covenant uniting bridegroom and bride, but 'bridegroom and bride' here refer inseparably to Christ and the Church and to this man and this woman."[2]

This new, covenantal relationship with the Blessed Trinity is effected by the Holy Spirit, bestowed through the Nuptial Blessing. "The covenant . . . is the Holy Spirit himself. He is the source of the unity of this undivided love; he is its divine bond, which human sin cannot break."[3] This work of the Holy Spirit is vividly expressed in the

---

1. Jean Corbon, The *Wellspring of Worship*, 2nd ed., trans. by Matthew J. O'Connell (San Francisco: Ignatius Press, 2005), 173.

2. Ibid.

3. Ibid.

Nuptial Blessing. The epiclesis asks the Lord to send down upon the couple "the grace of the Holy Spirit and pour your love into their hearts, that they may remain faithful in the Marriage covenant" (OCM, 74). Another form implores God, "Graciously stretch out your right hand over these your servants (N. and N.), we pray, and pour into their hearts the power of the Holy Spirit" (OCM, 207). The third form asks, "May the power of your Holy Spirit set their hearts aflame from on high" (OCM, 209). In the Sacrament of Marriage, as in every liturgical celebration, "the Holy Spirit is sent in order to bring us into communion with Christ and so to form his Body. The Holy Spirit is like the sap of the Father's vine which bears fruit on its branches" (CCC, 1108). This new relationship with the Blessed Trinity, guaranteed by God's own fidelity, endures for the whole of married life.

THE GRACE OF THE SACRAMENT OF MATRIMONY

The second principle effect of Marriage is the grace bestowed by the sacrament. Grace is the free gift of God that enables us to live out our vocation as his adopted children. Each sacrament imparts a special gift of the Holy Spirit that enables the recipients to live out the meaning of the sacrament. So this grace of the sacrament is also a distinctive relationship with the Blessed Trinity, for Christ himself is the source of this grace (CCC, 1642). "Just as of old God encountered his people in a covenant of love and fidelity, so our Savior, the spouse of the church, now encounters christian spouses through the sacrament of marriage" (GS, 48). This is an enduring encounter between Christ and the spouses, by which he "dwells with them, gives them the strength to take up their crosses and so follow him, to rise again after they have fallen, to forgive one another, to bear one another's burdens, to 'be subject to one another out of reverence for Christ,' and to love one another with supernatural, tender, and fruitful love" (CCC, 1642). Christ's abiding presence perfects the couple's love with his own love, strengthens their unity, and assists them in their growth in holiness and "in welcoming and educating their children" (CCC, 1641). The rite itself expresses this profound mystery: "In the union of husband and wife you give a sign of Christ's loving gift of grace, so that the Sacrament we celebrate might draw us back more deeply into the wondrous design of your love" (OCM, 200).

The language of grace and divine assistance permeates the Rite of Christian Matrimony. The Nuptial Blessing asks God to "send down upon them the grace of the Holy Spirit" so that "the grace of love and peace" would abide in the bride and that her husband would acknowledge her "as his equal and his joint heir to the life of grace" (OCM, 74). God is committed to supporting and sustaining marriage since he himself is its origin and source: "just as your goodness is its origin, may your providence guide its course" (OCM, 196). He is petitioned to be the guarantee of his own creation: "that the union you have created may be kept safe by your assistance" (OCM, 192). Likewise, his strength and protection are invoked so that the couple "may always be faithful in their lives to the covenant they have sealed in your presence" (OCM, 204). The Sacrament of Marriage is a unique and beautiful event that initiates a lifelong journey into the love and communion of the Blessed Trinity, brought about by the Holy Spirit, blessed by the Father, originating in Christ's love for the Church and sustained by his presence and grace.

Through this abiding presence God bestows "special gifts of grace and divine love" (GS, 49) that enable the spouses to live out all the aspects of marital love: the good of each spouse, openness to life, the gift and education of children, unity, indissolubility, and fidelity. Each of these elements brings about the holiness of the spouses and contributes to the effectiveness of their marriage as a sign of Christ's love for the Church. Although these dimensions of marital love are intrinsically intertwined, we will consider them separately, while suggesting the important interrelationships.

GOOD OF THE SPOUSES

From the beginning God intended marriage for the good of the spouses. In creating Adam he declared that "it is not good for the man to be alone. I will make a helper suited to him" (Gn 2:18). Drawn into a unique relationship with the Blessed Trinity through the Sacrament of Marriage, the "spouses are penetrated with the spirit of Christ and their whole life is suffused by faith, hope, and charity; thus they increasingly further their own perfection and their mutual satisfaction, and together they render glory to God" (GS, 48). However, this growth in holiness and the virtues is not without its own growing pains. St. Catherine of Siena's description of how all Christians grow in virtue speaks also to marital love. "You test the virtue of patience in yourself when your neighbors insult you. Your humility is tested by the proud, your faith by the unfaithful, your hope by the person who has no hope. Your justice is tried by the unjust, your compassion by the cruel, and your gentleness and kindness by the wrathful. Your neighbors are the channel through which all your virtues are tested and come to birth."[4] The spouses, persevering in their love for one another and sustained by the grace and power of the Holy Spirit, will assist one another to attain Christian maturity in humility, hope, compassion, justice, gentleness, and kindness.

As a sign of Christ's love for the Church, the spouses participate in Christ's sacrificial self-giving and assist one another in growing and persevering in this gift of self. The Apostle Paul applies this sacrificial love particularly to the husband: "Husbands, love your wives, even as Christ loved the church and handed himself over for her to sanctify her" (Eph 5:25). The model for the husband is Christ's gift of himself on the Cross to the Church. The Second Vatican Council included family and married life when it spoke of the laity's works, "For all their works, if accomplished in the Spirit, become spiritual sacrifices acceptable to God through Jesus Christ: . . . even the hardships of life if patiently borne (see 1 Pt 2:5)" (LG, 34). St. John Paul II applied this teaching on the whole of life as a spiritual sacrifice more specifically to spouses. "Just as husbands and wives receive from the sacrament the gift and responsibility of translating into daily living the sanctification bestowed on them, so the same sacrament confers on them the grace and moral obligation of transforming their whole lives into a 'spiritual sacrifice'" (FC, 56). All of this is contained in the simple question addressed to the couple by the priest as they prepare to declare their consent: "Are you prepared, as you follow the path of Marriage, to love and honor each other for as long as you both shall live?" (OCM, 60).

UNITY

At Creation God ordained unity as an essential aspect of marriage: "that is why a man leaves his father and mother and clings to his wife, and the two of them become one body" (Gn 2:24). This unity

---

4. Catherine of Siena, *The Dialogue*, trans. Suzanne Noffke, OP, Classics of Western Spirituality (New York: Paulist Press, 1980), 38.

contributes to the good of the spouses. Because they are no longer two but one, they "help and serve each other by their marriage partnership; they become conscious of their unity and experience it more deeply from day to day" (GS, 48). This unity is both an accomplished reality by virtue of the celebration of the sacrament and a lifelong process. This twofold reality is expressed in one of the Collects for Marriage:

> [P]our forth the help of your blessing . . .
> so that in the union of Marriage
> [these your servants] may be bound together
> in mutual affection,
> in likeness of mind,
> and in shared holiness. (OCM, 193)

United by sacramental grace, spouses grow together in affection, like-mindedness and holiness with the strength that comes from God's blessing.

 This twofold reality is also one of the petitions of the Nuptial Blessing:

> Grant, O Lord,
> that, as they enter upon this sacramental union,
> they may share with one another the gifts of your love
> and, by being for each other a sign of your presence,
> become one heart and one mind. (OCM, 207)

The union brought about through the sacrament comes to fruition in the course of their life together in a progressive "becoming" of one heart and mind. As the epiclesis of the sacrament, this petition in the Nuptial Blessing emphasizes the role of the Holy Spirit in bringing about and sustaining marital unity. St. John Paul II explains:

> The gift of the Spirit is a commandment of life for Christian spouses and at the same time a stimulating impulse so that every day they may progress towards an ever richer union with each other on all levels—of the body, of the character, of the heart, of the intelligence and will, of the soul—revealing in this way to the Church and to the world the new communion of love, given by the grace of Christ. (FC, 19)

 The all-inclusive nature of marital unity, embracing the soul, will, intelligence, heart, character, and body, highlights the important role that conjugal love plays in marital unity. Acts proper to marriage "are noble and honorable; the truly human performance of these acts fosters the self-giving they signify and enriches the spouses in joy and gratitude. . . . The unity of marriage, confirmed by our Lord, is clearly apparent in the equal personal dignity which must be accorded to man and wife in mutual and unreserved affection" (GS 49). In seeking "pleasure and enjoyment of body and spirit," the spouses "accept what the Creator has intended for them" (CCC, 2362). The marital act expresses the "free and mutual self-giving, experienced in tenderness and action, and permeates their whole lives; this love is actually developed and increased by its generous exercise" (GS, 49).

This unity, which results from free and total giving of self that is accomplished through the Exchange of Consent and fostered through the acts proper to marriage, includes both indissolubility and fidelity. This is so because marriage is a sign of God's faithfulness to his covenant and of Christ's fidelity to his bride the Church. The sacrament enables the spouses "to represent this fidelity and witness to it. Through the sacrament, the indissolubility of marriage receives a new and deeper meaning" (CCC, 1647). This is one aspect of the apostolate of marriage, for through their faithfulness spouses testify to the world "that God loves us with a definitive and irrevocable love" (CCC, 1648). The words of the seventeenth-century poet George Herbert retain their force today: "We live in an age that hath more need of examples than precepts."[5] Christian Marriage offers our contemporary world a much-needed sign of faithful love. The indissolubility of marriage is "a fruit, a sign and a requirement of the absolutely faithful love that God has for man and that the Lord Jesus has for the Church" (FC, 20).

The formulas for the Reception of Consent spoken by the priest express this indissoluble faithfulness. The first option asks, "May the God of Abraham, the God of Isaac, the God of Jacob, the God who joined together our first parents in paradise, strengthen and bless in Christ the consent you have declared before the Church, so that what God joins together, no one may put asunder" (OCM, 64). Fidelity is possible because husband and wife are joined, strengthened and blessed by God in Christ. The second option also asks the Lord to strengthen "in his kindness" the couple's consent "and graciously bring to fulfillment his blessing within you. What God joins together, let no one put asunder" (OCM, 64). Both options end by citing Christ's own admonition in

---

5. Izaak Walton, "The Life of Herbert," in *The Remains of That Sweet Singer of the Temple* (London: Pickering, 1841), xlvi.

Matthew 19:6: "Therefore, what God has joined together, no human being must separate."

Accepting the Gift of Life

Conjugal love achieves the twofold end of marriage, the good of the spouses and the transmission of life. Furthermore, the conjugal act itself has two inseparable meanings—unity and procreation. The fruitfulness of marriage was ordained by God as part of creation. He created mankind—male and female—in his image, blessed them, and said to them, "Be fertile and multiply" (Gn 1:27–28). In fulfilling this command, couples cooperate "with the love of God the Creator and are, in a certain sense, its interpreters" (GS, 50)—they "incarnate" the creative and fecund love of God, they say to the world, "This love is possible." In accepting "children lovingly from God" and raising them "according to the law of Christ and his Church" (OCM, 60), the Christian family reflects the creative work of the Trinity.

While the secular media often portrays the Church's teaching on the openness to life as being unrealistic and insensitive to the needs of the spouses, the Church does not wish to see couples exhaust themselves mentally, physically, or economically by having too many children too quickly. In fact Pope Paul VI goes into this in some detail, recognizing that spacing out births may be desirable due to the physical or psychological conditions of the spouses as well as external circumstances (HV, 16). Indeed, God himself has made provision for such circumstances, for he "has wisely disposed natural laws and rhythms of fecundity which, of themselves, cause a separation in the succession of births" (HV, 11). It is thus permissible "to take into account the natural rhythms immanent in the generative functions, for the use of marriage in the infecund periods only, and in this way to regulate birth" (HV, 16). In doing so, the spouses act as ministers "of the design established by the Creator" rather than its arbiters (HV, 13). Choosing to regulate births by means of the natural rhythms of the woman enriches the unity and communion of the spouses, for it recognizes "both the spiritual and corporal character of conjugal communion" by "accepting dialogue, reciprocal respect, shared responsibility and self-control" (FC, 32).

As a result,

conjugal communion is enriched with those values of tenderness and affection which constitute the inner soul of human sexuality, in its physical dimension also. In this sexuality is respected and promoted in its truly and fully human dimension, and is never "used" as an "object" that, by breaking the personal unity of soul and body, strikes at God's creation itself at the level of the deepest interaction of nature and person. (FC, 32)

The two meanings of the conjugal act, unity and procreation, are inseparable, "willed by God and unable to be broken by man on his own initiative" (HV, 12). Regulating births through contraception falsifies "the inner truth of conjugal love, which is called upon to give itself in personal totality" (FC, 32).

The conjugal act is intended by God to express spiritually and corporally the total gift of each spouse to the other. Contraception alters this profound expression of

"total" self-giving. Thus the innate language that expresses the total reciprocal self-giving of husband and wife is overlaid, through contraception, by an objectively contradictory language, namely, that of not giving oneself totally to the other. This leads not only to a positive refusal to be open to life but also to a falsification of the inner truth of conjugal love, which is called upon to give itself in personal totality. (FC, 32)

Spouses love one another not only for what each receives, "but for the partner's self," each rejoicing in being able to enrich the other with the gift of himself or herself (HV, 9).

In this gift of self, the Christian family is "a sign and image of the communion of the Father and the Son in the Holy Spirit" (CCC, 2205). This is how Jesus described Trinitarian self-giving, speaking of the Holy Spirit: "He will glorify me, because he will take from what is mine and declare it to you. Everything that the Father has is mine; for this reason I told you that he will take from what is mine and declare it to you" (Jn 16:14–15). All that the Father has is Christ's, and the Spirit takes that to glorify, not himself, but Christ. Conjugal love is a progressively more profound journey into the mystery of the Blessed Trinity.

The Education of Children

Accepting the gift of children brings with it the responsibility to educate them. It is a further participation in the creative activity of God, for "by begetting in love and for love a new person who has within himself or herself the vocation to growth and development, parents by that very fact take on the task of helping that person effectively to live a fully human life" (FC, 36). It springs from a proper appreciation of and indeed amazement at the enormity of the gift of life; an "awareness that the Lord is entrusting to them the growth of a child of God, a brother or sister of Christ, a temple of the Holy Spirit, a member of the Church, will support Christians parents in their task of strengthening the gift of divine grace in their children's souls" (FC, 39). This responsibility is "really and truly a 'ministry' of the Church at the service of building up her members" (FC, 38).

The Sacrament of Marriage is the source of and consecration for this ministry. It bestows both responsibility and gift. It bestows the responsibility "to share in the very authority and love of God the Father and Christ the Shepherd, and in the motherly love of the Church" (FC, 38). It equips them to assume this responsibility by enriching "them with wisdom, counsel, fortitude and all the other gifts of the Holy Spirit in order to help the children in their growth as human beings and as Christians" (FC, 38). The education of their children is rooted in the spouses' love for one another, a human love infused and elevated with Christ's love for his Church by the Sacrament. St. John Paul II explains: "As well as being a *source*, the parents' love is also the *animating principle* and therefore the *norm* inspiring and guiding all concrete educational activity, enriching it with the values of kindness, constancy, goodness, service, disinterestedness and self-sacrifice that are the most precious fruit of love" (FC, 36). These are specific aspects of the grace of the sacrament and the gift of the Holy Spirit, "the Gift that contains all gifts" (CCC, 1082).

In educating their children, the parents and the children together embark on "the path of a truly human training, of salvation, and of holiness" (GS, 48). The scope of education is all-inclusive, but the religious formation of their children is of primary importance. The parents are the "first heralds of the Gospel for their children" (FC, 39)—sharing with them the word of God, introducing them to prayer, teaching them concern for others, being examples of generosity and sacrifice, and bringing them into the Body of Christ through Christian initiation. By precept and example "they become fully parents, in that they are begetters not only of bodily life but also of the life that through the Spirit's renewal flows from the Cross and Resurrection of Christ" (FC, 39). Here again we see how the Paschal Mystery, the work of the entire Trinity, is the font of sacramental power.

Parents are also charged with educating their children in essential values. This includes the proper attitude toward material possessions expressed through a simple lifestyle that manifests the truth that each person is more precious for what he or she *is* than for what he or she *has* (GS, 35). It also inculcates a sense of justice that is understood as "respect for the personal dignity of each person" and the biblical understanding of love as a "sincere solicitude and disinterested service with regard to others" (FC, 37). A right understanding of justice and love form the basis for "a clear and delicate *sex education*" (FC, 37, italics original) that presents sexuality as "an enrichment of the whole person—body, emotions and soul—and it manifests its inmost meaning in leading the person to the gift of self in love" (FC, 37). This education is completed by formation in chastity, "the successful integration of sexuality within the person leading to the inner unity of the bodily and spiritual being" (CCC, Glossary). The entire educational process is a maturing and flowering of the total gift of self achieved through the Exchange of Consent and the consummation of the Marriage that grows and matures in family life. The family "finds in self-giving the law that guides it and makes it grow" (FC, 37).

Family Spirituality

"Christian spouses and parents are included in the universal call to sanctity. For them this call is specified by the sacrament they have celebrated and is carried out concretely in the realities proper to their conjugal and family life. This gives rise to the grace and requirement of an authentic and profound conjugal and family spirituality that draws its inspiration from the themes of creation, covenant, cross, resurrection, and sign" (FC, 56). Discuss how the themes of creation, covenant, cross, resurrection, and sign can be expressed in family spirituality. Review references to these themes in this chapter and chapters 7 and 8.

Missionary Vocation

The Lord also entrusts to the Christian family "an evangelizing and missionary task" (CCC, 2205), a theme that runs through the texts of the Rite of Marriage. Each of the Nuptial Blessings includes a petition that the couple would be Christian witnesses to the world, that they would "bear true witness to Christ before all" (Nuptial Blessing A), and "bear witness to you in the world" (Nuptial Blessing C). This theme is also expressed in the prayers for the wedding Mass. One of the Prayers after Communion asks that "those who are united by the Sacrament of Marriage may always hold fast to you and proclaim your name to the world" (Prayer after Communion, OCM, 211). A final example comes from the Solemn Blessing at the end of Mass:

> May you be witnesses in the world to God's charity,
> so that the afflicted and needy who have known your kindness
> may one day receive you thankfully
> into the eternal dwelling of God. (OCM, 77).

The Second Vatican Council described this dimension as the prophetic office of the family: "they must be witnesses of their faith and love of Christ to each other and to their children. The christian family proclaims aloud both the virtues of the kingdom of God here and now and the hope of the blessed life hereafter. Hence, by example and by their testimony, they convict the world of sin and enlighten those who seek the truth" (LG, 34). Christian Marriage manifests to the world not only Christ's *spousal* love for his Church, but also his *sacrificial* love for the world.

The Whole of Life

As we noted in the previous chapter, the Nuptial Blessings contain petitions for each of the spouses and for the couple together. These blessings further reveal the meaning of the Sacrament of Matrimony for the whole of life. The petitions for the bride ask that she "follow the example of those holy women whose praises are sung in the Scriptures" (OCM, 74) and that she would "bring warmth to her home with a love that is pure and adorn it with welcome graciousness" (OCM, 207). The petitions for the bridegroom ask that he "may be a worthy, good and faithful husband," and when appropriate, "a provident father" (OCM, 207). There also petitions for his relationship with his wife, that he may "entrust his heart to her," "acknowledge her as his equal and his joint heir to the life of grace," and cherish and honor her "with the love that Christ has for his Church" (OCM, 74). These prayers look ahead to the home and family that the couple will establish.

These individual petitions are enriched with several petitions for the couple. The Spirit is implored to help them persevere in the faith so that they will "hold fast to the faith and keep your commandments" and so "be blameless in all they do" (OCM, 74). The gift and blessing of children is found in all three Nuptial Blessings. Nuptial Blessing A asks that they would "be blessed with children, and prove themselves virtuous parents, who live to see their children's children" (OCM, 74). Nuptial Blessing B asks the Lord to "sustain . . . by their deeds, the home they are forming (and prepare their children to become members of your heavenly household by raising them in the way of the Gospel)" (OCM, 207). The third Nuptial Blessing asks that "living out together the gift of Matrimony, they may (adorn their family with children and) enrich the Church" (OCM, 209). Nuptial Blessing C looks ahead to the blessings and challenges of a long life together, asking that "In happiness may they praise you, O Lord, in sorrow may they seek you out; may they have the joy of your presence to assist them in their toil, and know that you are near to comfort them in their need . . . and after a happy old age, together with the circle of friends that surrounds them, may they come to the Kingdom of Heaven" (OCM, 209). Finally, through all these experiences, may they "share with one another the gifts of your love and, by being for each other a sign of your presence, become one heart and one mind" (OCM, 207).

CONCLUSION

Christian marriage is a sign of the Blessed Trinity and of Christ's self-giving love for the Church. It manifests in innumerable ways the faith of the couple. "Promising love for ever is possible when we perceive a plan bigger than our own ideas and undertakings," writes Pope Francis, "a plan which sustains us and enables us to surrender our future entirely to the one we love. Faith also helps us grasp in all its depth and richness the begetting of children, as a sign of the love of the Creator who entrusts us with the mystery of a new person" (LF, 52). The Christian family, a communion of persons blessed and sustained by God's faithful love, visibly expresses the Blessed Trinity, "a sign and image of the communion of the Father and the Son in the Holy Spirit" (CCC, 2205).

Chapter 10

The Sacraments of Vocation and at the Service of Communion: Conclusion

THE FAMILY: IMAGE OF THE TRINITY

Baptism, Confirmation, and Eucharist are the sacraments of Christian initiation. They establish all of Christ's disciples in their "vocation to holiness and to the mission of evangelizing the world" and confer on Christians the power to live "as pilgrims on the march towards the homeland" (CCC, 1533). The sacraments considered in this book, Holy Orders and Matrimony, are the sacraments of vocation since they confer the gift of the Spirit to live out a specific calling within the Body of Christ. The *Catechism* also refers to them as sacraments at the service of communion, since they "are directed towards the salvation of others" and "confer a particular mission in the Church and serve to build up the People of God" (CCC, 1534). The origin of the communion which they serve is the Trinity, for "the divine image is present in every man. It shines forth in the communion of persons, in the likeness of the unity of the divine persons among themselves" (CCC, 1702). The Sacraments of Holy Orders and Matrimony are at the service of this divine communion in distinct but complementary ways.

As a communion of persons, the Christian family is a sign of the Trinity, "a sign and image of the communion of the Father and the Son in the Holy Spirit" (CCC, 2205). The family, which the Church has described as the domestic church (LG, 11), is "the first and irreplaceable school of social life" (FC, 43), the first experience of communion. "The family is the place where different generations come together and help one another to grow in wisdom and harmonize the rights of individuals with other demands of social life; as such it constitutes the basis of society" (GS, 52). The family's "first and fundamental contribution to

143

society" is the daily experience of "communion and sharing" (FC, 43). Relationships within the family "are inspired and guided by the law of 'self-giving'; . . . this free giving takes the form of heartfelt acceptance, encounter and dialogue, disinterested availability, generous service and deep solidarity" (FC, 43). As we have seen in the previous chapters, generous self-giving manifested through dialogue, availability, and service, for example, are essential aspects of both the Sacrament of Holy Orders and the Sacrament of Matrimony. The sacraments of vocation are born and nourished in the family. It is in the family that individuals first hear God's response to the question, "How am I to serve God with my life?" "The education of children should be such that when they grow up they will be able to follow their vocation, including a religious vocation, and choose their state of life fully aware of their responsibility" (GS, 52).

MARRIAGE: COMMUNION OF LOVE

The self-giving experienced and learned in the family becomes the foundation for the Sacrament of Marriage. A man and woman bring to their marriage the communion they learned in the family. The communion between husband and wife, rooted "in the natural complementarity that exists between man and woman," grows through the willingness of the spouses to share "what they have and what they are" (FC, 19). Husband and wife "grow continually in their communion through day-to-day fidelity to their marriage promise of total mutual self-giving" (FC, 19). Thus conjugal communion "is the fruit and sign of a profoundly human need" that is confirmed, purified, elevated and led to perfection through the Sacrament of Marriage (FC, 19). "The Holy Spirit who is poured out in the sacramental celebration offers Christian couples the gift of a new communion of love that is the living and real image of that unique unity which makes of the Church the indivisible Mystical Body of the Lord Jesus" (FC, 19). This gift of the Spirit is both "a commandment of life" and "a stimulating impulse" that daily deepens marital communion and reveals "to the Church and to the world the new communion of love, given by the grace of Christ" (FC, 19).

Marriage is an indissoluble communion, "a small and precious sign" to the world "of the unfailing fidelity with which God and Jesus Christ love each and every human being" (FC, 20). This communion is rooted not in taking but in giving, "in the personal and total self-giving of the couple" (FC, 20). The Sacrament of Marriage offers the couple a "new heart," enabling them to overcome "hardness of heart" and "to share the full and definitive love of Christ, the new and eternal Covenant made flesh" (FC, 20). Marital communion is a sign to the world of God's love for men and women and for his Church, a love that is faithful to the end. Christ will not reject or be unfaithful to his bride, the Church. "If we are unfaithful he remains faithful, for he cannot deny himself" (2 Tm 2:13).

HOLY ORDERS: COMMUNION WITH THE MYSTERY OF GOD

The communion that is first experienced in the family is also the foundation for the Sacrament of Holy Orders. Christ came to gather into one those scattered by sin and the enemy (cf. Jn 10:12; 17:11, 21–23). Men who receive the Sacrament of Holy Orders participate in Christ's high priestly ministry of gathering the scattered children of God, imploring our merciful Father to "gather to yourself all your children scattered throughout the world" (Eucharistic Prayer III). This vocation too is rooted in the communion of the Trinity. "Through the priesthood which arises from the depths of the ineffable mystery of God, that is, from the love of the Father, the grace of Jesus Christ and the Holy Spirit's gift of unity, the priest sacramentally enters into communion with the bishop and with other priests in order to serve the People of God who are the Church and to draw all mankind to Christ in accordance with the Lord's prayer: 'Holy Father, keep them in your name, which you have given me, that they may be one, even as we are one . . . even as you, Father, are in me, and I in you, that they also may be in us, so that the world may believe that you have sent me' (Jn 17:11, 21)" (PDV, 12). For this reason, the ministerial priesthood is constituted "through this multiple and rich interconnection of relationships which arise from the Blessed Trinity and are prolonged in the communion of the Church, as a sign and instrument of Christ, of communion with God and of the unity of all humanity" (PDV, 12).

The source of communion for those who receive Holy Orders is episcopal communion. Each bishop is "the visible source and foundation of unity" in his diocese (LG, 23). In addition, "the bishops, the successors of the apostles, are joined together" (LG, 22), and they, "together with the pope represent the whole church in a bond of peace, love and unity" (LG, 23). The source of unity and communion for all is the Eucharist. "In any community of the altar, under the sacred ministry of the bishop, a manifest symbol is to be seen of that charity and 'unity of the mystical body, without which there can be no salvation' (St. Thomas Aquinas, *Summa Theologiae*, III, q. 73, a. 3)" (LG, 26). Priests "make the bishop present, in a sense, and they are associated with him in trust and generosity; for their part they take upon themselves his duties and solicitude and carry them out in their daily work for the faithful" (LG, 28). Deacons assist the bishop in the work of communion through the proclamation of the Gospel, "works of charity and functions of administration" (LG, 29).

CREATED FOR COMMUNION

Communion is written into the very nature of men and women. "The ultimate end of the whole divine economy is the entry of God's creatures into the perfect unity of the Blessed Trinity" (CCC, 260). The Sacrament of Matrimony serves this end by imparting to the spouses gifts of the Spirit that make their love fruitful, a love that deepens the communion between the spouses and welcomes the gift of children. The Sacrament of Holy Orders serves this ultimate end by participating in Christ's priestly work of gathering into one the scattered children of God. Both are fruits of Christ's prayer to his Father: "I in them and you in me, that they may be brought to perfection as one, that the world may know that you sent me, and that you loved them even as you loved me" (Jn 17:23).

FURTHER READING

Primary Sources: Collections

Benedict XVI. *Sacrament of Charity (Sacramentum Caritatis)*. Boston: Pauline, 2007.
   This is a rich and comprehensive discussion of the Sacrament of the Eucharist. It is divided into three main sections: "The Eucharist, A Mystery to Be Believed"; "The Eucharist, A Mystery to Be Celebrated"; and "The Eucharist, A Mystery to Be Lived." Also discusses the relationship of the Eucharist to each of the other sacraments and the Trinitarian dimension of the Eucharist.

———. *Verbum Domini (The Word of the Lord)*. Boston: Pauline, 2010.
   This excellent presentation of the Word of God is divided into three sections: "The God Who Speaks"; "The Word of God and the Church"; and "The Church's Mission: To Proclaim the Word of God to the World." Of particular interest for this book is the section entitled "The Liturgy: Privileged Setting for the Word of God."

Bishops' Committee on the Liturgy. *Introduction to the Order of Mass*. Pastoral Liturgy Series, vol.1. Washington, DC: United States Conference of Catholic Bishops, 2003.
   This resource is a good introduction to the Eucharist. Especially relevant to this book is the section entitled "The Eucharistic Celebration and its Symbols." This is a useful resource for all catechists.

Flannery, Austin, OP, ed. *Vatican Council II: The Basic Sixteen Documents*. Collegeville, MN: Liturgical Press, 2014.
   This is the classic collection of the sixteen major documents of the Second Vatican Council. Of particular interest for this book are the following documents:
   The Dogmatic Constitution on the Church, 20–29 (on bishops, priests, and deacons)
   The Pastoral Constitution on the Church in the Modern World, 47–52 (on Christian marriage)

John Paul II, *Familiaris Consortio (On the Role of the Christian Family in the Modern World)*. Boston: Pauline, 1981.
   This is a foundational text for understanding the Catholic teaching on marriage and the family.

Liturgy Documents, The. Vol. 1, 5th ed., and vol. 2, 2nd ed. Chicago: Liturgy Training Publications, 2012.

This is an excellent compendium of liturgical documents, including the *Constitution on the Sacred Liturgy* and general instructions for the sacraments. It is an invaluable reference tool for catechists.

Secondary Sources

Carstens, Christopher, and Douglas Martis. *Mystical Body Mystical Voice: Encountering Christ in the Words of the Mass*. Chicago: Liturgy Training Publications, 2011.

In addition to being an excellent resource on the Mass, part 1 is an excellent, easy-to-read overview of sacramental theology.

Corbon, Jean, OP. *The Wellspring of Worship*. Translated by Matthew J. O'Connell. 2nd ed. San Francisco: Ignatius, 2005.

This is a classic study of the liturgy by one of the principal authors of the section on prayer in the Catechism of the Catholic Church. Corbon's emphasis on the role of the Holy Spirit in the liturgy is particularly illuminating.

Daniélou, Jean, SJ. *The Bible and the Liturgy*. Notre Dame, IN: Notre Dame University Press, 1956.

This is an analysis of the liturgical language of the Sacraments of Baptism, Confirmation, and the Eucharist as well as the Sabbath as explained by the Fathers of the Church based on the Sacred Scriptures and sacred Tradition. This is an excellent resource for those interested in further study of mystagogical catechesis.

Haffner, Paul. *The Sacramental Mystery*. Herefordshire: Gracewing, 2007. (Available in the US from LTP.org.)

This is one of the best introductions to sacramental theology—concise, clear, and thorough. This is an excellent reference for all catechists.

Ratzinger, Joseph. *The Spirit of the Liturgy*. San Francisco: Ignatius, 2000.

This is a rich biblical, theological, and sacramental study of the liturgy. It includes discussions of the role of the Old Testament in the formation of the liturgy, the importance of sacred buildings and sacred time, sacred images and music, liturgy as rite, and the body and liturgy. This should be in the library of anyone interested in a deeper understanding of the liturgy.

INDEX